Good Practice Guide: **Mediation**

RIBA Good Practice Guides

Other titles in this series:

Building Condition Surveys, by Mike Hoxley

Employment, by Brian Gegg and David Sharp

Extensions of Time, by Gillian Birkby, Albert Ponte and Frances Alderson

Fee Management, by Roland Phillips

Inspecting Works, by Nicholas Jamieson

Keeping Out of Trouble, by Owen Luder, 3rd edition

Negotiating the Planning Maze, by John Collins and Philip Moren

Painless Financial Management, by Brian Pinder-Ayres

Starting a Practice, by Simon Foxell

Good Practice Guide:
Mediation

Andy Grossman, Centre for Effective Dispute Resolution

RIBA ⬛ **Publishing**

© Andrzej Grossman, 2009
Published by RIBA Publishing, 15 Bonhill Street, London EC2P 2EA

ISBN 978 1 85946 312 3

Stock Code 68700

British Library Cataloguing-in-Publication Data.
A catalogue record for this book is available from the British Library.

Publisher: Steven Cross
Commissioning Editor: James Thompson
Project Editor: Alasdair Deas
Designed by Ben Millbank
Typeset by Academic + Technical
Printed and bound by MPG Books, Cornwall

RIBA Publishing is part of RIBA Enterprises Ltd.
www.ribaenterprises.com

Author's dedication

This guide is dedicated to all CEDR staff, directors and consultants, present and past, who have established and continue to develop the field of mediation and conflict management.

Series foreword

The *Good Practice Guide* series has been specifically developed to provide architects, and other construction professionals, with practical advice and guidance on a range of topics that affect them, and the management of their business, on a day-to-day basis.

All of the guides in the series are written in an easy-to-read, straightforward style. The guides are not meant to be definitive texts on the particular subject in question, but each guide will be the reader's first point of reference, offering them a quick overview of the key points and then providing them with a 'route map' for finding further, more detailed information. Where appropriate, checklists, tables, diagrams and case studies will be included to aid ease of use.

Good Practice Guide: Mediation

There is great scope for reform of the construction industry, but it is unlikely that conflicts will be entirely eliminated, whether they be minor differences of opinion or full-scale contractual disputes. However, any approach to resolving such a conflict need not necessarily be antagonistic – it can also be seen as an opportunity for an open and equitable dialogue between the parties in dispute. This is the approach encouraged by mediation – one that is increasingly urged by the courts, referred to in contracts, and, importantly, one that can be used not only to resolve disputes, but also to prevent them from arising again in the future.

In this excellent introduction to the topic, Andy Grossman draws on his considerable experience as a mediator to demystify the process for architects and others in the construction industry, covering the practical aspects of engaging in and using mediation while also explaining the broader principles and concepts that encourage a fair and pragmatic outcome to the dispute.

In any architect's library, alongside guides to arbitration or adjudication, a little space should also be made for this slim but valuable volume.

Sunand Prasad
President, RIBA

Preface

For well over a decade, mediation has been a common means of trying to resolve commercial disputes. Before the introduction of the Civil Procedure Rules the Technology and Construction Court (or the Official Referees Court, as it was then called) adopted a policy of referring cases to mediation or expert determination. Many interventionist features of the practice of the Technology and Construction Court, including judicial case management, are now incorporated in the Civil Procedure Rules, under which the courts have had an obligation to encourage and enable the use of alternative dispute resolution (ADR), particularly mediation. The courts can stay proceedings for mediation to take place, and a party can be penalised in costs if it unreasonably refuses to try mediation. Also, the Pre-Action Protocol for Construction and Engineering Disputes, as with other pre-action protocols, places emphasis on avoiding litigation, giving a chance for the parties to agree a settlement before proceedings start. The protocol expressly requires the parties to consider at a pre-action meeting whether some form of ADR procedure would be more suitable than litigation.

Construction professionals cannot ignore the practice of mediation, whether they are advising their clients, find themselves in a problem or dispute with their client or are asked to participate in mediation.

This guide describes the use of mediation, not only as a process for dealing with claims and legal disputes but also as a key component of effective conflict management and dispute prevention. It addresses the practical aspects of preparing for, and participating in, a mediation.

Andy Grossman
May 2009

About the author

Andy Grossman, an architect by professional background, is a practising civil and commercial mediator and a Director of the Centre for Effective Dispute Resolution (CEDR), Europe's leading agency in providing mediation, training and conflict management services. His mediation experience covers general commercial, professional negligence, planning and construction cases. He has also acted as a facilitator and an independent chair in a number of contentious political environments to assist in negotiations between public authorities and external stakeholders on projects or to assist in improving team relationships and communications within major corporations.

Andy has been involved in the training of mediators in the UK and internationally and he regularly advises on the design of conflict resolution processes. Andy joined CEDR in 1999 and holds a Doctorate of Professional Studies in Commercial Mediation Development.

Contents

Introduction   xvii

**Section 1   Some preliminaries on settlement offers, litigation costs and
             funding**   **1**
             A litigation health warning   1
             Part 36 offers   3
             Assessment of costs   5
             Conditional Fee Agreements and 'after the event' insurance   6

Section 2   ADR choices   **9**
             Grouping ADR processes   9
             Assisted negotiation   9
             Evaluative methods of dispute resolution   10
             Adjudicative methods of dispute resolution   11
             Hybrids   11
             Key features of mediation   12
             Mediation and negotiation   13

Section 3   Preparing for mediation   **17**
             Typical structure   17
             When to mediate   18
             Choosing the mediator   19
             Co-mediation   21
             Documents   21
             The mediation agreement   22
             Mediation venue   23
             Site visits   23

Mediation fees 23

Who should attend the mediation? 24

Unrepresented parties 25

Authority to settle 25

Assistant mediators 26

Pre-mediation contact 26

Section 4   Engaging in mediation   29

Arrival and opening 29

Exploration 30

      Looking at the risks 30

      Loss aversion 31

      Sunk cost effect 32

      The illusion of control 32

      Attribution bias 32

      Hindsight bias 32

Bargaining 32

      Who moves first? 33

      Reactive devaluation 33

      Bottom lines 34

      Getting into deadlock 34

      Working groups 35

Conclusion 36

      Drafting the agreement 36

      Other outcomes 37

      No settlement 37

Section 5   Mediation examples   41

Variations and extension of time 41

Professional negligence 44

Planning 45

Public right of way 46

Section 6   Dispute prevention and conflict management   49

The cost of conflict 49

Managing the risk of disputes 50
Partnering 52
Contracts promoting principles of collaborative working 53
Non-escalation mechanisms and mediation 54
Enforcement of ADR clauses 56
PFI contracts 56
Arbitration or litigation as the last resort? 57
Dispute boards 58
Project mediation 60
Costs of dispute boards and project mediation 61

Appendices   **67**
  A   The courts' attitudes on refusals to mediate 67
  B   Model settlement agreement and Tomlin order 73
  C   Websites for further ADR-related information 77

References   **79**

Index   **81**

Introduction

The construction industry is complex in nature but simple to describe. It involves large numbers of project participants. It is susceptible to many external factors – political, legislative, technological and climatic. It has a fragmented workforce, often prone to skills gaps and shortages. Funding arrangements on certain types of project can be extremely complicated and the procurement process lengthy. Clients demand more and contractors run their businesses on wafer-thin margins. Is it any wonder, then, that there are so many opportunities for disputes to arise, and just as many opportunities for them to be handled badly?

Back in 1994, Sir Michael Latham published his report *Constructing the Team*. Its message was simple: through better teamwork, the construction industry could really deliver for its clients. The report was a rallying call for the reform of an industry described as 'ineffective', 'adversarial', 'fragmented', 'incapable of delivering for its customers' and 'lacking respect for its employees'. The Latham report triggered a raft of initiatives. It led to the establishment of the Construction Industry Board to oversee reform, and to Sir John Egan's 1998 report *Rethinking Construction*, which suggested that the industry adopt supply chain techniques successfully applied in other industries. To introduce and test radical improvements in best practice through particular projects, the Movement for Innovation was established, and later the National Audit Office report *Modernising Construction* of January 2001 encouraged the selection of contractors on the basis of value for money, the establishment of better relationships between clients and an integrated supply chain. All these initiatives promoted cooperative rather than adversarial management approaches to dealing with problems and improving 'bottom line' results. New and innovative forms of contract were published and 'partnering' became the new buzzword in the industry.

At the time of the Latham report most construction disputes in the UK were determined by litigation or arbitration. Arbitration was seen as having many advantages over litigation; in particular that the arbitrator was an expert in the subject matter of the dispute, allowing the arbitration to take place more quickly and efficiently compared with a judge conducting a hearing on a technical matter. But arbitration was seen as becoming increasingly burdened with the procedural formality of litigation, making it more time-consuming and costly than had been intended. Even the reforms in the 1996 Arbitration Act were not enough to halt the waning popularity of arbitration.

Instead, eyes turned to statutory adjudication under the Housing Grants, Construction and Regeneration Act 1996, which came into effect in May 1998. Adjudication, as proposed by Latham, was meant to reinstate some of the original intentions of arbitration.

Without doubt, adjudication has been used successfully to deal with disputes that would otherwise have taken on a life of their own. But statutory adjudication, like arbitration, is a legal dispute resolution process which does not take into account the parties' commercial and personal interests. Mediation provides an antidote to that.

Section 1
Some preliminaries on settlement offers, litigation costs and funding

In this Section:

- *A litigation health warning*
- *Part 36 offers*
- *Assessment of costs*
- *Conditional Fee Agreements and 'after the event' insurance*

A litigation health warning

Here is a true story.

Mr Burchell, a small builder, contracted to build two large extensions to the home of Mr and Mrs Bullard. The agreement provided for four stage payments. On 31 August 2000 the builder submitted his claim for the third stage payment for £13,540 after work to the roof had been done. This was never paid. Mr and Mrs Bullard were not happy with the work and wrote to Mr Burchell setting out what they said had to be done before any further payment would be made.

Letters were exchanged and each blamed the other for the difficulties. With £5000 worth of work left to complete, Mr Burchell left the site on 21 November 2000. Six months later he instructed solicitors, who wrote suggesting that to avoid litigation the matter be referred for alternative dispute resolution (ADR) through 'a qualified construction mediator'. The response from the Bullards' building surveyor was that 'the matters complained of are technically complex and as such mediation is not an appropriate route to settle matters'. The Bullards simply wanted Mr Burchell to complete the contract and make good the defective work.

On 5 February 2002 Mr Burchell began a court action for £18,318. The Bullards counterclaimed for £100,815. Of that sum £23,646 related to the roof, which the Bullards argued needed to be completely rebuilt. The litigation rumbled on and the case was eventually heard at the county court over five days in May 2004. The judge awarded Mr Burchell £18,327 plus costs on his claim and the Bullards £14,373 on their counterclaim. Mr Burchell, therefore, had a net win of £5000, which the Bullards were ordered to pay. But that was not everything. After four years of wrangling, Mr Burchell had spent £98,000 on legal fees and the Bullards £70,000. The question of who would pay the costs still remained. The judge ordered separate judgments on the claim and counterclaim. Mr Burchell should have the costs of the claim upon which he had been successful and the Bullards should have the costs of the counterclaim on which they had been partly successful. As a result, the recovery of £5000 by Burchell in court would cost him £136,000. In April 2005 the Court of Appeal took a look at the costs orders.

The Bullards had inflated their counterclaim, their expert was criticised and their surveyor's rejection of mediation was considered 'plain nonsense'. Mr Burchell admitted to making mistakes, but he was always willing to rectify his work and did not over-egg his claim.

The Court of Appeal disapproved of the Bullards' conduct in the lengthy litigation but stopped short of condemning them as having been so unreasonable that a costs sanction should follow many years later. The court considered the reasonableness of the Bullards' actions against the background of out-of-court settlement practice, which had not yet been established at the time litigation had started. Also, the defendants rejected the offer of mediation on the advice of their surveyor, not of their solicitor. Nevertheless, the Court of Appeal issued a stark warning that little sympathy would be shown in the future to those who disregarded mediation and battled on regardless. As for the Bullards, they were left paying their own costs, 60 per cent of Mr Burchell's costs and the costs of the appeal, totalling £145,000. So, £185,000 had been spent to secure a judgment of £5000 and the Bullards had to sell their house to pay the £250,000 legal costs. All that heartache and money on a dispute over a modest extension, which ultimately cost the Bullards the very thing they were investing in.

The story of Mr Burchell and Mr and Mrs Bullard offers a prompt to look at certain aspects of settlement offers, legal costs and legal funding since they are part and parcel of any negotiations between parties in legal disputes and, as is often the case in mediation, dealing with costs may become the final hurdle to jump before settlement. So before looking at ADR generally, and mediation specifically, there are a few basic but important points to keep in mind.

Part 36 offers

Part 36 of the Civil Procedure Rules provides a structure for making formal offers to settle disputes. A Part 36 offer enables one party to put pressure on another to bring litigation or threatened litigation to a quick end by establishing severe cost consequences where the claimant refuses an offer of settlement and then fails to beat the offer at trial or where the defendant refuses an offer of settlement and the claimant equals or beats the offer at trial.

A Part 36 offer, which is a 'without prejudice save as to costs' offer, can be made at any time, including before the start of proceedings and in appeal proceedings by a claimant or defendant. It can be made in respect of the whole or part of the claim, in respect of liability alone (leaving the amount of damages to be dealt with later), and in respect of counterclaims and any additional or third party (Part 20) claim.

Once a Part 36 offer has been made, there is a specified period called the 'Relevant Period' (which must be at least 21 days) in which to decide whether to accept or reject the offer. In most cases, permission is not required from the court to accept the offer. One exception is if the trial has already started and permission may be required if a claimant wishes to accept an offer made by one of a number of defendants.

Once the Part 36 offer has been accepted, and provided that it is made in respect of the whole claim, proceedings are automatically stayed on the terms of the offer. If the offer is for a sum of money, it must be paid within 14 days of acceptance of the offer, and the defendant will be responsible for paying the claimant's reasonable legal costs incurred up to the date of acceptance. If the offer was made less than 21 days before trial, the court will make an order as to costs.

If the offer is rejected, the case proceeds. The judge will not be aware of the offer until costs are to be determined, after judgment has been given.

An offer can be accepted after the Relevant Period (assuming it has not been withdrawn) but there will be additional costs consequences. A claimant who accepts an offer after the Relevant Period will be entitled to reasonable costs up to the end of the Relevant Period but will then be liable for the defendant's costs after that date. A defendant who accepts an offer after the Relevant Period will be liable for the claimant's reasonable costs up to the date of acceptance.

Consequences of not accepting a Part 36 offer

For the claimant

If the claimant gets more than the defendant's offer at trial, the offer is immaterial and the claimant will get costs as normal.

If the claimant fails to beat the defendant's offer, the claimant will only recover costs up to the end of the Relevant Period. From that point the claimant will then have to pay the defendant's costs (plus interest) up to the end of trial and bear its own costs in that period.

For the defendant

If a defendant rejects a claimant's offer and the claimant gets less than the offer at trial, the offer is immaterial and the claimant will get costs and interest.

But, if a defendant rejects a claimant's offer and the claimant equals or beats the offer at trial, the defendant will be penalised for not accepting what proved to be a reasonable offer. The defendant will be ordered to pay damages and, unless the court considers it unjust, the claimant will get (1) interest on damages and costs at up to 10 per cent above base lending rates and (2) 'indemnity costs' rather than 'standard basis costs'.

Normally, the court only awards standard basis costs (see below). These are usually between 50 and 70 per cent of the legal costs a party has incurred and must be proportionate to the issues in dispute. Indemnity costs significantly increase the percentage of recoverable costs (which can be as high as 90 per cent) and there is no ceiling on proportionality.

Assessment of costs

At the end of a trial, or at an interim stage before trial, the court will order the basis upon which costs will be paid. The general rule at the end of a trial is that 'costs follow the event', which means the unsuccessful party pays the costs of the successful party.

Different costs orders can be made at the end of an interim stage. These include the following:

- *Costs in the case* – the unsuccessful party pays the successful party's costs at the end of the proceedings.
- *Costs reserved* – the decision regarding costs is deferred until a later time, but if no later order is made the costs will be costs in the case.
- *Costs in any event* – costs payable irrespective of whether the paying party wins or loses the claim.
- *No order as to costs* – each party bears its own costs of the proceedings to which the order relates whatever costs order is made at the end of the proceedings.
- *Claimant's/defendant's costs in the case/application* – if the claimant/defendant is successful, the other party will pay the successful party's costs, but not if the other party is successful.
- *Costs thrown away* – where a party is allowed to change its position on an issue in the case, the other party is entitled to the costs it has unnecessarily incurred as a result.
- *Costs of and caused by* – where a party amends its claim and the other party must amend its response, the other party is entitled to the costs incurred in amending its response.
- *Costs here and below* – where a party is entitled both to the costs of the proceedings in which the court makes the order and to the costs of proceedings in any lower court.
- *Wasted costs order* – an order against a solicitor or barrister whose conduct has led to unnecessary costs.

Where a costs order has been made, the court will assess how much of the successful party's legal costs should be paid by the unsuccessful party. The parties can agree what costs should be paid, but if they are unable to agree they must go through the assessment procedure, which may be either by way of detailed assessment (at the end of a trial) or summary assessment (at an interim stage before trial).

Even a successful party will usually have to pay a proportion of its legal costs as only a proportion is recoverable from the unsuccessful party. An unsuccessful party will have to pay all its own costs (unless a Conditional Fee Agreement is in place – see below) and a substantial proportion of the successful party's costs.

The order for costs may be assessed in the following ways:

- *Standard basis* – for most circumstances the court only allows costs that are proportionate to the matters in issue and will decide whether the costs were reasonably incurred or reasonable and proportionate an amount in favour of the unsuccessful party. The successful party will typically recover between 60 and 70 per cent of its costs.
- *Indemnity basis* – where a party is penalised for misconduct or as a result of a claimant beating a Part 36 offer the court will assess costs without reference to proportionality and any doubt as to whether the costs are reasonably incurred is resolved in favour of the successful party. The successful party will typically recover between 70 and 80 per cent of its costs.

Conditional Fee Agreements and 'after the event' insurance

A Conditional Fee Agreement (CFA) is an agreement between lawyer and client where the lawyer's fees are based on the outcome of the litigation. It is often referred to as a 'no win, no fee' agreement. If the claim is unsuccessful at trial, the lawyer charges a reduced fee, or sometimes no fee. If the claim is successful, the lawyer charges a 'success fee' on top of normal fees. The unsuccessful party usually pays the success fee, but not always in full.

The success fee can be up to 100 per cent of the lawyer's normal fees and is calculated by the lawyer's risk analysis of the case. The success fee cannot be a percentage of damages awarded or agreed in settlement before trial.

The unsuccessful party can have the success fee assessed by the court. The court can also allow different success fee percentages for different elements of costs or for different periods during which costs were incurred.

If the successful party has a CFA in place and/or 'after the event' legal expense insurance (see below), such costs may include the success fee and/or insurance premium.

The existence of the CFA must be disclosed to the other party (or parties) at the start of litigation proceedings, and the risk assessment must be disclosed to the court and, if necessary, to the other party (or parties) when costs are assessed.

'After the event' (ATE) insurance indemnifies the insured's disbursements and the costs and disbursements of the other party if litigation proceedings are discontinued or lost at trial. It can be purchased before or after the start of litigation proceedings.

The solicitor acting for the insured will be required to report regularly to the insurance company on the progress and developments in the case, particularly if any offers are made by the other party to settle the case.

SUMMARY

Settlement offers, litigation costs and funding

Part 36 offers
- Part 36 offers can be made at any time to put pressure on another party to bring litigation to a quick end.
- Such offers are 'without prejudice save as to costs'.
- Not accepting a Part 36 offer may significantly affect a party's costs following a judgment.

Assessment of costs
- At the end of litigation, the court will determine how the costs are to be calculated and apportioned.
- Generally, the unsuccessful party pays the costs of the successful party.
- A successful party will usually have to pay a proportion of its legal costs.

Conditional Fee Agreements
- So-called 'no win, no fee' agreements.
- The existence of a CFA must be disclosed to all other parties at the start of litigation proceedings.

'After the event' insurance
- Indemnifies the insured's disbursements and the costs and disbursements of the other party if litigation proceedings are discontinued or lost at trial.

Section 2
ADR choices

In this Section:

- *Grouping ADR processes*
- *Assisted negotiation*
- *Evaluative methods of dispute resolution*
- *Adjudicative methods of dispute resolution*
- *Hybrids*
- *Key features of mediation*
- *Mediation and negotiation*

Grouping ADR processes

ADR refers to all dispute resolution processes outside litigation where a third party assists in the resolution of a dispute. ADR can be used in addition to or alongside litigation or other proceedings as well as being an alternative.

One way of grouping ADR processes is to look at the degree to which parties have control of the process and outcome (Figure 2.1). The processes can be grouped into three categories:

- assisted negotiation
- evaluative methods
- adjudicative methods.

Assisted negotiation

- *Mediation* – a structured negotiation process managed by an independent third party (the 'neutral') with the aim of leading to a legally binding outcome; the subject of this guide.
- *Conciliation* – a process similar to mediation but sometimes distinguished by the feature that the neutral can put forward a solution or terms of settlement.

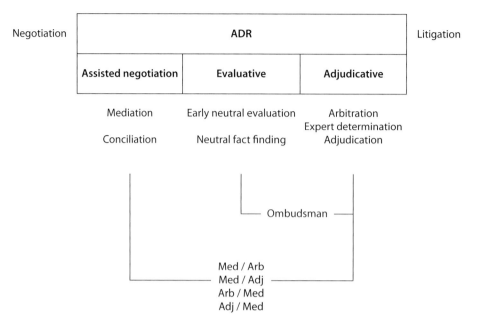

FIGURE 2.1: *Categories of ADR processes*

The Advisory, Conciliation and Arbitration Service (ACAS), for example, distinguishes conciliation from mediation as a process in which the neutral issues a written recommendation. However, the term 'mediation' is increasingly used to cover the full spectrum of third party facilitation techniques, irrespective of the extent to which the neutral is actively involved in proposing settlement terms.

Evaluative methods of dispute resolution

- *Neutral fact finding* – a neutral investigates factual, legal or technical issues and submits a non-binding report to help the parties reassess their respective positions. The parties agree in advance how the results of the process will be used. For example, they could agree to be bound by the findings, or they could agree to use the findings to negotiate a settlement. Neutral fact finding is often used in conjunction with other ADR processes.
- *Early neutral evaluation* – an evaluator gives an opinion on the likely outcome at trial or in relation to other expert judgments to help to progress further negotiations or settlement discussions or as a precursor to mediation.

Adjudicative methods of dispute resolution

- *Adjudication* – the Housing Grants, Construction and Regeneration Act 1996 provides a statutory right to adjudication. The Act sets out the features of a compliant adjudication procedure, which, among other features, requires the adjudicator to act impartially and to reach a decision within 28 days. It also allows the adjudicator to take the initiative in ascertaining the facts and the law. The decision of the adjudicator is binding unless or until the dispute is finally determined by court proceedings, arbitration or by agreement of the parties.

  Parties can design their own contractual procedures as long as they are compliant with the Act. If they do not comply or the contract does not mention adjudication, the Scheme for Construction Contracts (England & Wales) Regulations 1998 provide a statutory adjudication procedure that acts as a default mechanism. A number of ADR providers have produced their own adjudication rules.
- *Expert determination* – an independent expert with inquisitorial powers gives a final and binding decision on a technical or financial dispute. The expert can make investigations independently of the parties and does not need to refer back to the parties before arriving at the decision. There is no statutory right of appeal. Provided the expert has answered the right question and has decided the right issue, the decision will be enforceable.
- *Arbitration* – a formal, binding process, regulated by the Arbitration Act 1996, where the dispute is determined by the arbitrator or panel of arbitrators on the basis of a legally reasoned award. In contrast to litigation, arbitration is seen as more readily enforceable across international boundaries and may give the parties more control over procedure, timing and the appointment of the third party arbitrator. Although subject to challenge on limited grounds, the award is rarely subject to appeal.

See also: Arbitration or litigation as the last resort?, page 57

Hybrids

- *Ombudsman* – for maladministration in areas involving citizen or consumer complaints. It is a variant of adjudication and usually involves a case appraisal preceding the decision of the ombudsman.
- *Med-Arb/Med-Adj* – a mediation with a provision for the dispute to be referred to arbitration or adjudication for a binding decision if the mediation does not

result in a settlement. The process is meant to encourage parties to arrive at their own settlement under the threat of one imposed by an arbitrator or adjudicator. The parties may choose to have the same person act as both the mediator and the arbitrator or adjudicator, or for one person to be the mediator and another the arbitrator or adjudicator. There may be a difficulty if the same person acts in both roles as the parties may be more guarded in revealing their needs and vulnerabilities in the knowledge that the mediator may eventually act as arbitrator or adjudicator.

- *Arb-Med/Adj-Med* – the arbitrator or adjudicator arrives at a binding decision and invites the parties to negotiate through mediation. If the parties turn down the invitation or are unable to reach a settlement for themselves, the decision is revealed. (The Centre for Effective Dispute Resolution (CEDR) *Rules for Construction Adjudication*, for example, provide for mediation to be used in this way.)
- *Dispute prevention* – in contrast to ad hoc dispute resolution, where the neutral is asked to intervene at the point where a dispute arises, other mechanisms allow for neutrals to be appointed at, and involved from, the start of the project. The intention is to ensure that the neutral is not only familiar with the project but is also in a position to deal with problems as they arise. The principal mechanisms are described in Section 6 of this guide.

The RIBA offers a number of these dispute resolution options to the construction industry, including mediation, adjudication, expert determination and arbitration.

Key features of mediation

CEDR defines mediation in the following way:

> Mediation is a flexible process, conducted confidentially in which a highly skilled impartial person actively assists parties to work towards a negotiated agreement of a problem or dispute, with the parties in ultimate control of the decision to settle and the terms of resolution.

Mediation avoids the procedural rigidity of litigation and offers remedies and relationship outcomes that are not available from adversarial processes. Unlike a court, which imposes a decision on the parties based on its assessment of which party is to blame for the situation in which the parties find themselves, mediation allows for options that can deal with the parties' commercial and personal interests, aiming to achieve the outcome best suited to the parties' needs.

Mediation has a very different communication dynamic from that found in a court or tribunal. In court, a party's task is to persuade the judge of its case. It addresses its arguments, through the barrister, to the judge and not to the other side. The client is detached from the exchanges between the other side, judge and witnesses (unless the client is a witness himself). Arguments are presented in a public arena, in a set-piece format.

In mediation, parties present to each other; the party representatives are at the heart of discussions, supported by their professional advisors. The confidentiality of private meetings means that the parties can talk frankly and openly – about the case, their weaknesses and strengths and their view of their opponent's case – without fear that what they disclose will be shared with the other side. The 'without prejudice' status of mediation means that no information disclosed during the mediation, including the details of any settlement offer, can be used as evidence in any subsequent court or other proceeding.

In addition, the dynamics can be changed to suit the circumstances of the conflict. For example, establishing working groups on a particular task, having a meeting only with senior executives or meeting with individuals only. Mediation therefore allows for the best combinations of people to meet and for meetings to run in parallel. This can be a real advantage in disputes involving a number of parties or people.

Mediation and negotiation

As mediation is an assisted negotiation, recognising the way in which people negotiate is the starting point for describing how and why mediation works as an effective way of resolving problems and disputes.

At its simplest, negotiation is a discussion between two or more parties who are trying to resolve their problem. Negotiations happen because the parties want to create something new that neither can achieve on its own or to resolve a dispute between them. They recognise that they have conflicting interests and hope to use some form of influence to get a better deal, rather than accepting what the other party will voluntarily give them.

While the search for an agreement is a common goal, the parties will not usually want or need the same thing. One party may try to push the other to accept its demands, try to persuade the other party to change its position and compromise or come up with a solution that both parties can live with.

SUMMARY

The key features of mediation compared with litigation

LITIGATION	MEDIATION
Adversarial	**Consensual**
Parties engage as combatants with a binding decision imposed by the judge	Parties agree to negotiate a solution with the help of a mediator. Outcome rests with the parties
Compulsory and binding process	**Voluntary and non-binding process**
Rules, procedural rigidity	Models, flexibility
Lawyer-centred	**Client-centred**
Rights focused	**Interests focused**
Only addresses legal obligations of the parties or legal interpretation	Can address legal rights and commercial and personal interests. Parties retain their rights if no settlement is reached
Retrospective analysis	**Present/forward looking**
How the parties have ended up where they are and who is to blame	How the parties have ended up where they are and what they can do about it
Relationships damaged or destroyed	**Relationships maintained or repaired**
All or nothing settlement	**Range of options**
Legal remedy available only	Solutions not limited by legal rules or precedent
Public	**Confidential**
Hearing generally open to the public and exposed to media coverage	Parties agree extent of confidentiality

Section 3
Preparing for mediation

In this Section:

- *Typical structure*
- *When to mediate*
- *Choosing the mediator*
- *Co-mediation*
- *Documents*
- *The mediation agreement*
- *Mediation venue*
- *Site visits*
- *Mediation fees*
- *Who should attend the mediation?*
- *Unrepresented parties*
- *Authority to settle*
- *Assistant mediators*
- *Pre-mediation contact*

Typical structure

Mediation is a fluid process. Exactly how a mediation is conducted will depend on the type of case, the parties, the content of the dispute and the timing before trial or other statutorily based determination process.

Most mediations are conducted in a day, and although there are many shapes to mediation it is convenient to describe the process as involving five phases (Figure 3.1), consisting of any number or combination of joint and private meetings.

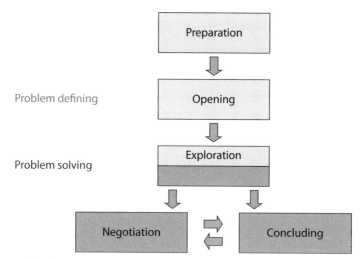

Problem defining

Problem solving

FIGURE 3.1: *The five phases of a mediation*

When to mediate

No construction dispute is inherently unsuitable for mediation. However, construction disputes are complex and often a dispute related to a small part of the works can lead to serious and far-reaching consequences unless a solution can be found quickly. The decision regarding when to mediate, therefore, needs to be made after considering the effects of any delay.

If mediation is undertaken at an early stage and while the project is still under construction, there is a greater likelihood of finding a commercial resolution before costs start to build up and the parties harden their positions. In addition, the parties will be able to control many more issues and be able to 'trade' their claims. If a dispute continues until after construction is complete, usually the only resolution the parties are negotiating for will be a purely monetary one.

Another reason to consider mediation at an early stage is the opportunity it affords to learn about the case or emerging claims. That is not to say that mediation should be used simply as a fishing expedition. However, even if the mediation does not reach a settlement, it may help the parties to focus their case or narrow down the issues between them. The parties can always try mediation later.

In any event, the Civil Procedure Rules and the related Pre-Action Protocol for Construction and Engineering Disputes compel all parties to examine a case fully, even though there may be no certainty that proceedings will be issued if settlement is not reached and no guarantee of recovering such investigative costs if the claim does not proceed.

Nevertheless, there may still be reluctance to engage in mediation at an early stage of the dispute or before litigation has started. One party may feel that there has not been enough pain for the other party through, say, threatening proceedings to show that it means business. Also, if insurers have been notified of a potential claim they may not be convinced about pre-litigation discussions because the claim has not been fully articulated.

The decision to mediate early is a trade-off between, on the one hand, cost and time saving and the avoidance of entrenched attitudes and, on the other hand, incompleteness of information and frustrated negotiations. At the very least, this means having an understanding of the strengths and weaknesses of the claim and the BATNA.

A party may believe that the more information it has, the more control it will have over the outcome of the mediation and the greater likelihood of the mediation 'going their way'. The party may therefore feel that it does not have enough information to enable it to form a view as to the right level at which to settle at mediation. However, it should take care not to delay mediation through a quest for perfect information. It is not unusual that the first day of mediation is just the start of the mediation process and that additional information may still be required before a final settlement can be reached.

Choosing the mediator

Increasingly, independent mediators who practise full time or, more commonly, practise alongside their primary profession accept direct instructions to act as mediator. This will invariably mean that the parties already know the mediator they want. Alternatively, a mediator can be chosen through a mediation service provider.

There are many mediation service providers in the UK. Most of them are accredited by the Civil Mediation Council, which requires accredited providers to have minimum standards of training and continuing professional development for their mediators.

Because service providers generally obtain detailed feedback on the performance of their mediators they can readily match a mediator to the particular needs and characteristics of a particular dispute. They can make the process of agreeing on the mediator easier because they recommend a mediator, rather than each party having its 'own' candidate.

If the other party does propose a mediator it has worked with before, that is no reason to immediately object to that mediator. Remember, the mediator has no power to pressure a party to agree to anything it does not want to, and if the other party is proposing a mediator, it is probably doing so because it believes the mediator has the ability to settle the case.

In a particularly complex case, a shortlist of mediators can be identified and a joint 'beauty parade' can be held to decide who should be selected.

Whichever route is taken to selecting the mediator, mediators must be selected on a consensual, rather than a least objectionable, basis. The important thing to keep in mind is that no two mediations are the same. The personalities will be different and will respond to different types of mediator. It is not enough for the mediator to understand the legal and technical issues. He or she must understand how to relate to the parties sufficiently to bring them to a resolution they are both willing to live with.

Some mediations may require the mediator to have the gravitas and authoritative voice that comes from many years of experience. Others may require a persuasive and personable mediator with strong interpersonal skills and an ability to see the big picture. If the dispute is emotionally charged, the mediator will need to be comfortable with handling emotional parties and able to gently guide the case to a settlement. If the parties are more abrasive and intransigent, they will need logic and tenacious persuasion.

It is also undoubtedly the case that construction disputes require the mediator to have some familiarity with the subject matter. Saying that, however, does not mean that the mediator must be an expert. Subject matter expertise is less important than expertise in the process of mediation.

While settlement is the goal of mediation, asking about the mediator's settlement rate is rarely useful on its own. There are many complex variables involved in whether a dispute settles or not, and it is difficult to isolate those variables so that they relate neatly to aspects of the mediator's performance.

There is also no evidence to suggest that either lawyers or non-lawyers make better mediators.

Co-mediation

Some cases, particularly multiparty cases, can benefit from having two mediators working together. Two mediators will be able to combine their different skills and areas of professional expertise and can achieve a balance between parties and mediators – for example, evening out cultural, ethnic or gender differences. By working in tandem, two mediators can keep parties more fully and efficiently engaged; by working with more than one party at a time they can cut down on the amount of time parties are not occupied, which inevitably occurs when a mediation is conducted by only one mediator. The management time saved can easily outweigh the additional cost of co-mediation.

Documents

Ahead of the mediation, each party will prepare a case summary and send it to the mediator and to the other party at an agreed date. The case summaries are usually exchanged simultaneously.

Preparing the case summary, which will normally be five to ten A4 sheets, is an important exercise in focusing parties on the real issues in dispute and any non-legal matters which should be considered if they are to reach a settlement. It is not uncommon that copies of pleadings are sent to the mediator in place of case summaries. However, pleadings are limited to the extent that they focus solely on the legal aspects of the dispute. They are not an adequate substitute for a succinct case summary.

The case summary should include the following:

- a chronology of the events leading up to the dispute and the negotiation history, including details of settlement offers
- the court/arbitration timetable, if any
- the names of the people involved in the dispute
- details of the claims and counterclaims
- the areas that are not in dispute or have been agreed prior to the mediation
- references to key points in the supporting documentation, such as experts' reports.

It is also open for a party to send the mediator a confidential briefing paper mentioning issues that would be awkward to include in its case summary – for example, difficult personalities and relationships which could present a problem at the mediation or threaten a settlement. Similarly, a party may want to send the mediator a particular document in confidence, such as a draft expert's report.

Almost always the summaries will be accompanied by a bundle of supporting documents. As construction disputes are notorious for the amount of detail they produce, there may be a temptation to provide the mediator with substantial documentation. However, it is worth remembering that settlement in construction disputes is rarely achieved by spending much time discussing detail. More likely than not, this would have happened before the mediation, and may be the very reason why parties have reached deadlock.

Where possible, a joint bundle should be agreed between the parties to avoid duplication.

The mediation agreement

Mediation is conducted subject to a formal mediation agreement, which provides for confidentiality and states that the parties will not call the mediator as a witness in any proceedings. In addition, the mediation will be held on a 'without prejudice' basis, which means that all communications made for the purposes of the mediation will not be admissible in court proceedings, though the fact that mediation has taken place is not in itself inadmissible.

"a mediation settlement … is enforceable by legal proceedings"

Under English law, as long as a mediation settlement constitutes a contract, it is enforceable by legal proceedings just as any other contract. Although contracts usually require no formalities to be completed to make them enforceable, mediation agreements commonly provide that no settlement will be binding on the parties unless in writing and signed by, or on behalf of, the parties.

The structure of a mediation agreement is typically as follows:

- reference to the mediation procedure and mediator code of conduct
- authority and status of the signatories
- confidentiality and without prejudice status of the mediation

- settlement formalities, i.e. settlement not being binding until put in writing and signed by the parties
- mediation fees, legal and other costs
- legal status and effect of the mediation
- changes (if any) to the agreement and/or mediation procedure to which the agreement refers.

Mediation venue

Most mediations now take place at the offices of one party's lawyers. This has the advantages of not having to pay for an alternative venue and being easier to arrange. Sometimes, however, parties will not want to mediate in the other lawyer's or other party's office in the belief that the other party will gain an advantage by working on their own territory. This is a matter of a party's own perceptions rather than a likely outcome. It is not the neutrality of the venue that counts but the neutrality of the mediator.

If the parties are geographically distant from one another then a venue halfway between them may be more equitable in terms of travel time and costs. The location of the mediation venue will also need to take into account whether a site visit is to take place on the day.

Site visits

A site visit may be valuable to the mediation, particularly if there has been no opportunity for an inspection or where the dispute revolves around workmanship and defects issues. A visit for the mediator on his or her own may also be useful to put the dispute into context.

If a party suggests a site visit, the mediator will want to establish what that party hopes to achieve by it. It may be that the visit is not appropriate for the approach or level at which the parties want to negotiate.

If a site visit is to go ahead, it must be seen as a part of the process and not an afterthought. This means consideration needs to be given to timing, who is to attend and whether any negotiation is anticipated to take place on the site.

Mediation fees

Some mediators charge an hourly rate. Others charge a lump sum fee based on the value of the dispute, or a day rate with preparation time charged at an hourly rate. Preparation time includes reading of the documents, making arrangements for the mediation day itself (unless that is done by a mediation service provider) and pre-mediation discussions. Additional fees will include time spent on any follow-up work, including finalising any settlement agreement or assisting the parties to continue discussions if the mediation day did not result in settlement.

Where a mediation service provider is used, it may charge a separate referral fee.

Usually the parties will share the mediation fees and disbursements equally and bear their own costs and expenses in attending the mediation. Some procedures provide for the parties to claim mediation fees as 'costs in the case' if the dispute proceeds to trial, or the parties can choose to opt out of this provision.

Who should attend the mediation?

The effectiveness of any mediation will depend on having the right people at the table. This starts with having a senior representative of each party who has the authority to settle, followed by the party's legal advisor. Beyond that it is necessary to bring along only those people who will genuinely assist the negotiation of a settlement or help to explain any difficult factual or technical issues. For example, if the dispute involves a valuation issue, the presence of a quantity surveyor at the mediation would be beneficial. However, it may not be necessary for the quantity surveyor to be present for the entire day: only up to the point that all questions falling within his or her area of knowledge have been answered.

Often parties will insist on bringing their experts. From a mediator's perspective the presence of experts is looked upon with some caution. More often than not, each party will have an expert who has produced a report that gives a different interpretation and conclusions from other experts. Those conclusions are very unlikely to change to the extent that it will affect the mediation.

If experts do attend the mediation, the mediator may need to address the reason for any differences between the experts' opinions and adapt the process to make the presence of the experts as productive as possible. For example, the mediator may ask the experts to work together to identify common ground between them or to narrow or agree certain issues. The mediator may also ask them to take part in a session in which each expert asks the other a limited number of questions in front of the mediation teams. This allows each team to hear the best case of the other and to assess how their expert witness might come across in court.

In the situation where an employer is claiming against a contractor, consultants present as a member of the employer's team may feel that the mediation could expose them to a potential professional negligence claim. With that threat in mind, those consultants are likely to be highly defensive in their approach. How much they will be able to contribute positively to the mediation, therefore, needs to be considered carefully. Also, just because one party has decided to attend the mediation with, say, a barrister or expert does not mean the other party (or parties) must do the same.

The best approach is to keep the number of people attending the mediation to as few as possible, and to have others available on the telephone if required. The smaller the mediation team, the more involved and effective it is likely to be.

Unrepresented parties

Sometimes, parties in domestic construction disputes, particularly claimants in professional negligence cases and cases involving unpaid fees, choose for financial or other reasons to attend the mediation without legal representation. The mediation service provider (if one is involved) and the mediator will check with unrepresented parties whether a lawyer has been advising them before the mediation and, if a lawyer has been involved, whether they will have access to the lawyer during the mediation.

When an agreement is reached at the mediation, it is written down and signed by all parties, becoming a binding contract. Signing such an agreement can have implications for a party's legal rights. An unrepresented party may request, or the mediator may suggest, a breathing space of a few days to seek appropriate legal advice and to confirm the acceptability of any draft agreement reached at the mediation.

Authority to settle

The mediator will check with the parties before the mediation whether they have authority to settle at the mediation. However, in most cases party representatives are unlikely to have unlimited authority. Typically, a representative from an insurance company or the insurer's solicitors will have a predetermined limit.

Before the mediation, the mediator may ask whether a party's authority to settle extends only up to the level of offers previously made or whether the authority is for the full amount of the claim. The mediator may also ask whether the representatives can obtain additional discretion, if it is required, in order to take into account any new information or perspectives and unexpected developments that may arise over the course of the mediation.

A representative may be required to speak to a senior colleague or other colleagues not present at the mediation to seek approval to go beyond their limit of authority or to receive approval for proposals. In this situation, the mediator will want to ensure that those colleagues are contactable, particularly outside normal working hours. Also, the mediator may insist that the other party is made aware of any strict limits.

There may be circumstances where some representatives come with very limited or no authority. For example, representatives of local authorities and other public bodies may only be able to participate in the mediation on the basis that any potential settlement would be 'recommended for approval' by the representative and conditional upon subsequent approval by the relevant board or committee. All the parties would need to be aware of this before the mediation.

A related issue is that, in some cases involving public bodies, it may be difficult to impose full confidentiality on the mediation process because of a statutory requirement for scrutiny by the National Audit Office, the Public Accounts Committee or public consultation or because of media pressure.

Assistant mediators

The mediator may bring along, unless the parties object, an assistant mediator. The assistant is trained but has little experience. The assistant attends as an observer to gain greater exposure to mediation and to learn from experienced mediators. The assistant may be allowed to take a more active role at the discretion of the mediator and can provide additional professional expertise without additional cost to the parties.

The confidentiality provisions of the mediation agreement apply to the assistant.

Pre-mediation contact

Before the mediation the mediator will be in telephone contact with the parties' lawyers. The same confidentiality rules of mediation communications will apply to pre-mediation contact.

During pre-mediation contact the mediator will cover:

- how the parties have arrived at mediation
- who will be attending
- the assistant mediator
- any comments or concerns the parties have about the process of the day
- opening presentations
- the mediation agreement, and whether any changes have been proposed and agreed by all the parties
- the personalities involved
- the content and context of previous settlement discussions and offers to settle, including Part 36 offers (see Section 1)
- court timetable
- costs to date and to trial (including whether the lawyer is acting under a Conditional Fee Agreement – see Section 1)
- authority issues
- questions related to the case summary, supporting documents and any confidential briefing papers
- venue, start time and any time restrictions on the day for party representatives.

In a multiparty case, the mediator will want to confirm the negotiation approach the claimant and the defendant group will be taking in the mediation. For example, in a dispute in which the employer seeks damages from the contractor and subcontractors for faulty workmanship, will the employer make a separate demand on each member of the defendant group or will it make one demand and leave it to contractor and subcontractors to negotiate among themselves how that demand will be met? If a global settlement of the dispute cannot be achieved with the defendant group, will the employer settle with one party?

Similarly, have the contractor and subcontractors determined they should negotiate as a group with the employer and make a joint offer of settlement and, if so, how far have they been able to agree the contribution percentage each will be willing to make?

In complex cases where the defendants are at odds on the issue of contribution, the mediator may suggest having a separate day of mediation with only the defendants. A second mediation day can be scheduled with all the parties to resolve the case as a whole.

SUMMARY

Preparing for mediation

Preliminary contact with the mediator (or the mediation service provider) to confirm:

- date and duration of the mediation
- latest date of receipt, or simultaneous exchange, of case summaries and supporting documents
- the terms of the mediation agreement
- venue
- mediation fees
- party representatives and authority to settle.

Confidential follow-up telephone calls for the parties to address concerns about the mediation, and for the mediator to ask questions related to the case summary and supporting documents.

Possibly a pre-mediation meeting with all parties to agree points of process.

Section 4
Engaging in mediation

In this Section:

- *Arrival and opening*
- *Exploration*
- *Bargaining*
- *Conclusion*

Arrival and opening

The mediator will usually arrive at the venue ahead of the parties to check facilities and room locations and to decide on who will sit where in the main meeting room, particularly if many parties are attending. When people arrive, the mediator will show them to the room designated to their group, where they can work and keep their documents throughout the day.

Before the joint opening meeting, the mediator will meet the parties in their rooms, asking them to sign the mediation agreement and making sure they have no concerns before the mediation gets under way. The mediator will give everyone enough time to prepare, and will then bring the parties together in the main meeting room.

At the opening meeting, at which all the parties will be present, the mediator will briefly remind them of his or her role and the process, and then invite them to make their opening presentations. During contact with the parties before the mediation, the mediator may have reminded the parties of the importance of the opening presentations and that, for them to have some impact, they should not be regurgitations of the pleadings. Even so, opening presentations often revert to a positional bargaining approach and try to reconstruct the whole project, describing every issue in great detail.

Because construction mediations cover many issues, prioritising the issues is essential. Unless the parties are seeking a global settlement from the start, some detailed discussion will be expected on each of the issues. If the parties have not identified the issues they wish to discuss before the mediation, in the opening meeting the mediator will list the issues and, with the parties, prioritise them or decide on the order of discussion. Where many parties are involved, a timetable for meetings can also be agreed. Doing this exercise reminds the parties that there is simply not enough time to discuss every issue in detail (particularly as most construction mediations are scheduled for one day) and helps to encourage everyone to look more broadly at a potential settlement and spend less time getting bogged down in the detail.

Exploration

During private meetings, the mediator will examine the important issues and needs of each party, and discuss differences in understanding of fact, expert opinion or likely legal outcome.

Different arrangements can be devised to settle a construction dispute in mediation because the settlement need not be monetary in nature. A settlement can involve a contractor performing a repair (although there is the possibility that this could lead to another dispute), putting a contractor on the shortlist for another job, or dismissing certain claims or counterclaims with no money changing hands. For example, a contractor may be less interested in money than in having additional time to complete the job or in obtaining future work, while the owner may want the project completed as quickly and as economically as possible.

Looking at the risks

See also: Assessment of costs, page 5 — The assessment of litigation risk attempts to predict the outcome of a judgment set against the cost of pursuing or defending a claim and the costs which will be recoverable if the party wins its case.

Often, parties give considerable weight to their lawyers' views of the prospect of success at trial, or at least see their lawyers' views in an excessively favourable light. A lawyer may say that a case is 'quite strong' and attach to it a 70 per cent chance of success (which means it has a 30 per cent chance of failure!). A party representative may perceive this as a 90 per cent chance of success.

The mediator will focus the attention of a party on the strengths and weaknesses of both its own case and the other party's case and will want to understand the parties' positions in other potential risk areas, including the following:

- *Commercial risk* – what commercial options could be factored into a settlement and what happens if the dispute fails to settle?
- *Personal risk* – what might be the impacts on personal reputation and future working relationships?
- *Reputational risk* – what might potential outcomes mean for different stake-holders, suppliers and the employer?
- *Regulatory risk* – could any impending or potential changes in the regulatory environment affect a potential settlement?

Uncertainties in the prediction of risk can be exposed by the mediator, who will be sensitive to a number of biases that may give a party a distorted view of its own case and position. In other words, the mediator can reveal how different forms of bias adversely affect a party's behaviour.

Loss aversion

Imagine you are offered a bet on the toss of a coin: if the coin comes up heads, you have to pay £100. What is the minimum you would need to win if tails comes up to make this bet attractive? Most people say somewhere between £200 and £250, showing that an expected loss typically has about two and a half times the impact of a gain of the same magnitude. The reason for the strength of this bias is that loss is associated with the feeling of responsibility and associated blame, which we seek to avoid. People tend to make risk-averse choices when facing a gain; that is, they prefer small guaranteed gains to larger but riskier ones. People facing losses, however, tend to make risk-seeking choices; that is, they prefer riskier outcomes to sure losses.

In the context of negotiation and mediation, claimants generally face an assured gain in settlement or the possibility of a larger gain at trial or arbitration. In the absence of counterclaims, defendants face an assured loss by settling or the potential of a bigger loss at trial.

Sunk cost effect

Once we have made an investment, whether in money, effort or time, we often feel the need to defend it vigorously. Because an investment has been made, it is necessary to get a return on it. Although we know that our investment is, or may have been, misjudged, we resist acknowledging that we may have made a mistake. This makes it difficult when negotiating, because we are unable to escape the shackles of past investments through fear of the humiliation of admitting to bad judgment.

The illusion of control

The more control people feel they have over an outcome, the more they become confident in its success, and the more overly optimistic they become about the likelihood of desired outcomes. This over-optimism is often sustained in negotiation teams, where individuals support each other and 'group think' develops.

Attribution bias

This bias occurs when we attribute a person's actions to our perception of what type of person they are, rather than to the situation influencing that person's actions. Often, in a negotiation, one party's inability to move towards a successful outcome will be based on its belief that the other party cannot be trusted or is, somehow, to blame. To minimise the effect of the bias, the mediator can look into the background of the other party's situation or ask how the first party would have behaved in a similar situation.

Hindsight bias

We often hear people say 'I always new that would never work'. Once something has happened we believe that it was predictable. Making sense out of what we are told about the past seems so easy that we tend to override previously stored memories, making it difficult to reconstruct past experiences. The effect of this is that we tend to view past decisions by others as wrong, whereas those decisions may have been more than reasonable given the information available at the time.

Bargaining

Parties coming to mediation will have different levels of negotiation experience and negotiation skill. For that reason the mediator can be seen to act as a negotiation coach, helping the parties to evaluate the effect of a planned demand or offer or helping them make meaningful offers at the right time.

Who moves first?

As the parties move from exploration and dispute analysis to bargaining, they are faced with either making the first offer or waiting for one from the other party. Parties in a mediation often believe that the opening offer should come from the other party in the belief that it will provide valuable information about its negotiating position and will give an indication of what type of settlement would be acceptable. This makes sense, but it ignores the impact that first offers have on how parties think about the negotiation.

Research and experience strongly suggest that first offers, together with an explanation of their basis, often set the tone for the discussions to follow and can give an accurate indication of the bargaining range in which a settlement could be achieved. Our minds tend to give disproportionate weight to the first information we receive when we are required to make decisions. In negotiation, this means that first offers strongly anchor subsequent thoughts and judgments.

Because first offers have power, the mediator will work to discourage a party making an overtly aggressive offer as part of positional negotiation tactics. The offer has to be reasonable enough for the other party to consider that a settlement is possible.

"first offers strongly anchor subsequent thoughts and judgments"

Reactive devaluation

Sometimes there are certain things one person does not want to hear from another, even if they are favourable. A party may become suspicious of the other in the belief that there will be a catch, or that the offer does not match the value of the concession sought.

As an offer moves from an exploratory potential offer to a formal one, the value of the offer decreases, and it may be rejected in the belief that its terms only strengthen the other party's position. For example, a building owner may propose remedial works on a project and reject a contractor's alternative proposals even though the contractor's proposals may be more technically sound and cost-effective.

People tend to devalue what seems to be readily available and place more value on what they do not have or cannot get. Offers from the opposing party are often valued less than the same offer made by a mediator.

Bottom lines

Mediators do not ask for bottom lines because they know they can change as the mediation continues. When a party announces that a particular number is a bottom line or best and final offer, invariably what they really mean is that they have not yet been persuaded or given enough information to change that position.

Of course, the announcement of a bottom line can be a bluff or an attempt to scare the other party; but sometimes it is real. The mediator will explore what further information or circumstances would make that party review its bottom line. This may mean re-examining the risks the party may face if the dispute is not settled, looking to see what else the party can offer by way of a concession to arrive at what it needs, assessing the impact of further information from the other party or all of these options.

With new information a party is free to make a new decision. This allows people to save face and back down from the bottom line statement by giving them a legitimate reason to move a little further. This will also apply in circumstances where a party in a multiparty mediation is paying more attention to what another party is offered than to whether its own offer serves its needs. For example, in a construction claim where there are a number of co-defendants contributing to a global settlement, one defendant might take a position that is entirely dependent on another defendant's offer by saying that it will contribute the same amount as the other defendant but no more.

Getting into deadlock

The potential for deadlock is present in any negotiation; it is sometimes inevitable, sometimes unexpected and sometimes deliberate. The most common reasons for getting into deadlock include the following:

- *Entrenchment* – parties become entrenched in their positions, conceding nothing or refusing to concede more. Similarly, lawyers and other advisors might feel the need to protect their client, urging clients not to concede too early, or to hold onto an extreme position in an attempt to get the other party to bargain against itself.

- *Moving too soon* – a party may believe that its bottom line has been exposed too early, leaving it little or no room to manoeuvre. When one party stops at an early stage, even if a reasonable offer has been made, the other party may see this as not negotiating properly and feel that the first party is not negotiating in good faith.
- *Emotional blockage* – a party may have a reputation to make or maintain, it may hold onto a position as a matter of principle, it may fear failure, or it may simply dislike the other party or members of its own team.
- *Team dynamics* – in particular, there may be a temptation to 'grandstand' in front of colleagues to impress and gain approval.
- *Tactical deadlock* – a deliberate delay to put pressure on the other party to concede more.
- *A need to save face* – a party's senior representative may refuse an offer or proposal not because it is inherently unacceptable, but because they want to avoid the feeling or the appearance of giving in to the other side. They may also want to avoid the embarrassment of looking weak in front of their own negotiation team.

The mediator has to find a way to break the deadlock. A number of options are available, including:

- bringing the senior party representatives together
- changing the negotiation teams
- breaking down big issues into smaller ones
- moving the parties away from the detail and making them take a wider perspective
- reminding the parties on how much progress has been made, either in individual meetings with each party or in a joint meeting
- asking the parties to take a break
- having a brainstorming 'anything goes' session.

Working groups

During the course of the mediation, the mediator may ask to see different combinations of people or may put together working groups on specific tasks while private meetings are taking place. Working groups might comprise:

- lawyers from each party
- experts from each party

- party principals alone
- surveyors/project managers/engineers from each party.

If the mediator has an assistant (which is advisable in multiparty cases), the assistant may be asked to sit in on working group meetings while the mediator works with other groups or parties.

Working groups may be established to clarify or gain further information, to discuss specific options for settlement or as a strategy to break deadlock.

Conclusion

Having reached a point where the bare bones of a settlement have been agreed orally, the mediator will work with all the parties so that they can draft the settlement agreement, which will become binding once it is signed. Even though everyone is tired and eager to go home, the agreement needs to be recorded in reasonably full terms so that difficulties do not arise later.

Drafting the agreement

Although a mediator may help to draft the agreement, typically the mediator will ask the lawyers to jointly draft it themselves. The mediator will check the draft for clarity and, with the parties, consider whether the agreement:

- is workable
- addresses all the issues in dispute
- is free from any obstacles to implementation
- reflects lessons learnt from the original dispute
- provides a timetable for events or actions, e.g. date for payment or schedule of payments
- deals with tax issues, e.g. VAT
- deals with legal costs
- specifies default conditions, e.g. interest on late payments.

See also: Appendix B – Model settlement agreement and Tomlin order, page 73

Where court proceedings are in place, the lawyers may want to draft a Tomlin order (a consent order made by a court staying an action on terms agreed by the parties and set out in a schedule to the order). A model settlement agreement and Tomlin order is given in Appendix B.

Other outcomes

While the aim of mediation is to reach a binding agreement that is clear and comprehensive, a mediation may conclude with other possible outcomes. Other outcomes include:

- an interim agreement
- a conditional agreement (likely where one of the parties is a public body and its representatives do not have discretionary authority to settle on the day and must seek final confirmation, either by senior colleagues or by way of a recommendation subject to committee approval)
- adjournment
- no settlement.

No settlement

If settlement is not reached, it is usual for the mediator to convene a joint meeting at the end of the day with all participants (or at least the lawyers) to review progress made and the areas that remain in dispute. This primarily allows the mediator to plan how further discussions between the parties might be taken forward.

It is very rare for a mediation to have achieved nothing, and many cases that do not settle on the day will settle within a few days or weeks, sometimes with the further help of the mediator. Pressure to settle undoubtedly builds up as the mediation day continues. If a dispute has run for a long time, it may be very difficult for a party to let it go in one day: the party may experience 'settlement panic' as discussion of settlement options take place. If there has been a considerable gap between the parties, it will take a lot of

"It is very rare for a mediation to have achieved nothing"

closing, and that may not be possible in one day, or even a series of days. Even when mediation has not prevented a trial, it is often found that it has narrowed the issues substantially and reduced costs overall.

While mediation has been described here in the context of settling disputes, as a decision-making process, it can also be used to:

- prevent and manage conflict

- define precisely problems in dispute, for subsequent referral to settlement mediation or another dispute resolution process
- negotiate contracts, where the process is used to manage procedures during negotiations and to improve communications generally.

SUMMARY

Engaging in mediation

Opening

Initial joint meeting at which:

- the mediator clarifies the process and establishes the ground rules
- the parties present a summary of their case to each other
- issues are clarified/identified.

Exploration/bargaining

Private, confidential meetings between the mediator and each party separately to:

- examine the important issues and needs of each party
- make the case clear to enable the mediator to articulate it when meeting the other party
- encourage openness about the weaknesses and strengths of their own and the other party's case
- discuss the effect of non-settlement on subsequent litigation
- discuss options for settlement.

Exploration/bargaining/conclusion

Joint meetings as appropriate at which parties may:

- set the agenda
- negotiate directly
- discuss differences in understanding of fact, expert opinion or likely legal outcome
- involve a meeting of experts or subgroups on specific issues
- agree a possible adjournment
- record the mediation outcome in writing, which may take the form of:
  - a signed settlement agreement on the day, which forms a binding contract
  - a conditional agreement, such as a draft heads of agreement or letter recommending approval
  - a settlement set out in the form of a schedule made the subject of a Tomlin order
  - a statement giving areas that are or are not in dispute
  - an agenda for further mediation.

Section 5
Mediation examples

In this Section:

- *Variations and extension of time*
- *Professional negligence*
- *Planning*
- *Public right of way*

The following sections give examples of mediations conducted by the author. Non-construction-specific examples have also been included to show the diversity of application and flexibility of the process.

Variations and extension of time

The dispute concerned the valuation of variations and the award of an extension of time on a college sports facility project. The parties had already attempted to resolve the dispute through direct negotiations but were still apart by £1 million when the mediation took place. The content and tone of the negotiations were made known to the mediator in his contact with the parties before the mediation, which had been set for two consecutive days.

The employer's team consisted of the principal of the college, the architect, the building services consultant, the structural engineer and the quantity surveyor, who was the lead negotiator. The contractor's team consisted of the regional director, the commercial director, the contracts manager, the site agent and the site quantity surveyor. No solicitors were present.

Before the first joint meeting the mediator asked the two quantity surveyors to agree the figures in dispute, which he put on a flipchart, and whether any other discussions had taken place just before the mediation. The quantity surveyors said that some progress had been made but that both sides were still substantially apart. Nevertheless, the figures in dispute were identified and agreed.

At the joint meeting it appeared that there was a good relationship between the college principal and the contractor's directors. However, there was much defending of positions by various parties involved in the day-to-day running of the project.

Due to the substantial amount of detail in the case, both parties agreed, at the request of the mediator, to go to their rooms to come up with three areas of claim that they considered required more significant discussion. However, this would take place after discussion of the extension of time in the joint meeting. The mediator then had brief private meetings with each party to agree the agenda for the next joint session and allowed them time to prepare what they wanted to say.

The mediator gave the parties one hour to present and discuss their points, during which many comments were directed at individuals around the table. Both principals, however, after intervention by the mediator, agreed to move on. The session had been useful, but neither party believed it had really heard anything new. Both the contractor's regional director and the commercial director became frustrated because they had moved in their position since the start of the mediation but had not heard anything from the employer's team to suggest that it showed a similar willingness to move.

After lunch, the mediator held a series of private meetings with each party examining some of the points that had emerged from the previous joint meeting. It became apparent that the college principal needed something to justify him moving from his current position. The mediator discussed some of the points that could possibly cause difficulties with the college's board of governors if a settlement was not reached at the end of the mediation. It also became apparent that the presence of some of the consultants was blocking progress of the discussions, so the mediator decided to focus his attention on the principals. He tasked the quantity surveyors to discuss two key items, one at a time, and to report back to their respective teams and the mediator.

During the meeting between the quantity surveyors, the mediator discussed potential settlement figures with the lead negotiators. The college principal confided to the mediator that he had authority to settle at a certain limit and that if agreement was going to exceed that limit he would have to obtain sanction from the governors. Although the principal was reluctant at first to go back to the governors, the mediator reminded him that the contractor had moved in the mediation from the figure put on the flipchart in the morning. The college principal acknowledged this, although maintaining the contractor had moved from a previously unacceptable position.

As the relationship between the principals had generally been good, the mediator prepared the college principal to explain the situation regarding the governors to his counterpart, the contractor's regional director. In the meeting that followed, the college principal and the contractor's directors agreed with the mediator that the mediation should be adjourned and reconvened four weeks later, by which time the college principal would have met with the governors.

A schedule of tasks to be completed before the mediation was reconvened was agreed by the parties, with the mediator to monitor progress. It was also agreed that the reconvened mediation should last a half-day, with only the decision-makers attending: two people on each side.

Four weeks later, the college principal had obtained a significant increase in his level of authority, but explained in a joint meeting that this really was his limit and that it would not be possible to go back for more money. During the course of the half-day most of the discussion took place in joint session, with the parties now being £150,000 apart. However, in a private meeting with the mediator, the college principal confirmed that the gap would still be £100,000, even if he stretched to his maximum authority to settle. The mediator then went to the contractor's directors to say that as the employer had moved from a difference of £1 million to £100,000, they should review their position in this light or face the risk of both parties returning to previous positions. In particular, the mediator stressed that the college governors had effectively sanctioned the increase in the financial limit to finally settle the dispute.

The contractor's regional director was reluctant as he, too, would find it very difficult to justify to his other directors what would be seen as giving away another £100,000. However, he did want to settle and so the mediator asked him whether he wished to consult with another senior executive. The regional director confirmed that he wanted to clear the additional £100,000 with his managing director, but that he was away until the next day. The mediator then asked the college principal to make his offer of settlement. Knowing that the offer would have to wait for consideration until the next day, the mediator asked the parties to draft a settlement agreement which they could review with their lawyers beforehand.

The next day the regional director telephoned the mediator to say that the employer's offer had been accepted and that the lawyers were now fine-tuning the agreement.

Professional negligence

The claimant, a wealthy businessman, alleged that an architect had negligently administered a refurbishment contract for his house and had failed to supervise the works adequately. Defective works had not been rectified, but the builder had been paid in full and had left site. The architect admitted a failure to obtain planning permission for some external works, but denied that the work had been so defective as to justify not issuing a certificate of practical completion. The architect also maintained that the builder would, but for the claimant's conduct, have returned to site to deal with what were relatively minor defects.

Participants in the mediation included the claimant, his lawyer and his expert, and the architect, the lawyer acting for the architect's insurer and their expert.

In the opening joint meeting, the lawyers gave predictably bullish opening statements, at the end of which the mediator asked the parties to say what they thought would be impediments to a settlement. The question prompted several matters to be raised, which were agreed to be issues between the parties that required discussion.

In the first private meetings it became clear that the claimant and the builder had finished up on very bad terms. The architect felt aggrieved that the claimant had insisted on the use of this builder, but acknowledged that on the whole he had been satisfied with the standard of the builder's work. He also said that the planning permission issue, to which he had already admitted, had led to only a small loss.

As there was still considerable difference between the experts, it was agreed that they could usefully address the issues of the extent of the defective work and the costs involved in making good the defects. They were called back to a meeting with the mediator to report on progress before finally reporting to their respective clients, and subsequently to a joint meeting with all present.

The mediator then asked to see the lawyers individually to get a feel for the potential settlement range. The experts then reported they had achieved a considerable level of agreement on the value of the work, although they disagreed on the value of the remedial work still outstanding and whether the scope of the work would require the claimant to vacate the property. The effect, nevertheless, was to reduce the claimant's expectations considerably.

No offers to settle had yet been made.

At this point, the mediator had a private meeting with the claimant to see whether he would now be in a position to make a first offer. Reluctant at first, the claimant finally agreed, making an offer reasonable enough to engage the attention of the lawyer for the architect's insurer. A settlement was eventually reached after an exchange of four counteroffers.

Planning

The mediation concerned the refusal of planning permission to develop and refurbish a listed building owned and used by a trust as a home for people with learning disabilities. The building was a substantial grade 2* listed 18th century house set in a landscaped park and had been subdivided to provide bedsit units. Four modern buildings within the park grounds provided additional units.

The trust wanted to develop new accommodation and found a development partner to build new facilities. This released the main house for conversion and refurbishment without the trust having to use its own funds. An architect prepared a scheme and submitted plans to the local planning authority.

Despite it being recommended for approval by the planning officer, the planning committee refused permission for the development. The trust had prepared an appeal but had not yet lodged it with the Planning Inspectorate, hoping to avoid the appeal by trying mediation.

Participants in the mediation included a director of the trust, a senior planning control officer, a regional inspector from English Heritage, the architect for the trust and the developer, a representative from the parish council, a local councillor and three representatives from the local residents group.

Having received all the case summaries, the mediator had substantial telephone contact with the parties before the mediation. The mediator also arranged to meet one of the directors of the trust at the house to see the site. In particular, the mediator wanted to persuade the trust not to attempt to present an alternative proposal at the opening session of the mediation.

Beginning with a joint meeting, all parties, in turn, presented their views and identified the key planning issues. These were listed as: the interior of the main house, the new buildings, the setting of the house, traffic, parking and access, preservation of trees, protection of wildlife and the general viability of the proposal. The trust was also keen to show the financial restrictions it was working under.

The joint meeting soon exposed the residents' antipathy towards the planning officer and hostility towards the developer as this was the first time the proposal had ever been explained in detail. It emerged that a number of invitations to representatives of the residents group to attend presentations made by the architect had been ignored, which came as a surprise to the local councillor.

After a single private meeting with each party, the mediator prepared the parties for a final joint meeting. At this meeting the trust's architect proposed a potential reconfiguration of the site and design alterations to the main house. The new proposal was accepted in principle and further meetings were agreed with English Heritage and the planning officer to enable the trust to make a new planning submission, which the planning officer was prepared to recommend for approval.

Public right of way

The dispute involved objections to a number of extinguishment orders and a creation order across farming land in five ownerships.

The owner of a farm, an isolated private dwelling surrounded on all sides by public footpaths, went to the district council to discuss proposals for changes to the footpaths. Before making an application to the council, the owner worked with the neighbouring farmers to come up with a proposed route that would be acceptable to them all and to the council. The council was proactive in its approach. Despite various concerns and alternative suggestions offered by the Ramblers' Association, the owner made an application for changes to the footpaths, resulting in a package of extinguishment orders and a creation order. The owner and the council believed that the changes offered greater privacy and security and would enable more efficient farming of the arable land. In addition, the new route was more direct and less intimidating, with easy-to-follow, wider paths with a firmer surface.

However, two objections remained from the Ramblers' Association. The first related to a proposed increase in road walking from the next nearest public right of way, and the second related to the drafting of the orders.

Despite trying to overcome the objections, the council felt unable to progress matters. Meanwhile, the applicant and the farmers were becoming increasingly frustrated, particularly as they had been able to agree a new footpath route. The council, therefore, proposed mediation, to which all the parties agreed.

Before the mediation, the mediator contacted the parties to gauge their understanding of the dispute, what problems they each thought they would have to confront and overcome, and the extent to which the council, the applicant and the neighbouring farmers were speaking as one. The mediator also addressed the technical objection to the drafting of the orders with the council and the Ramblers' Association so that the issue would not be used as a means of posturing at the mediation.

Subsequent negotiation at the mediation was influenced by a number of factors, including:

- the personal involvement and investment of time by the Rights of Way Officer, whose post was being made redundant and who was therefore determined to have the dispute settled
- the representative and negotiator for the Ramblers' Association working in the shadow of his senior colleague, who was a recognised expert in rights of way matters
- one of the farmers owning substantially less land than the others
- the council entering the mediation assuming it was speaking for the applicant and the farmers
- one of the farmers hoping to build on his land, a scheme for which planning permission was almost certain never to be granted, and, more generally,
- the principled objections of the Ramblers' Association set against the practical considerations of the landowners.

The mediation lasted for five hours, at the end of which the parties agreed to a modification on the creation order. However, the mediator was concerned that one of the farmers, who was worse off financially than the other landowners and was having to bear an increased responsibility for the agreed route, should have the opportunity to speak to family business associates. The farmer was given time to contact his brother to confirm acceptance of the compensation being offered by the council for the additional length of proposed footpath over his land to cover for the loss of crop area. After a positive telephone call, the council recorded the outcome and actions agreed in the mediation by way of a memorandum. The Ramblers' Association agreed to formally withdraw its objection in writing.

Section 6
Dispute prevention and conflict management

In this Section:

- *The cost of conflict*
- *Managing the risk of disputes*
- *Partnering*
- *Contracts promoting principles of collaborative working*
- *Non-escalation mechanisms and mediation*
- *Enforcement of ADR clauses*
- *PFI contracts*
- *Arbitration or litigation as the last resort?*
- *Dispute boards*
- *Project mediation*
- *Costs of dispute boards and project mediation*

The cost of conflict

The end product of a construction project always belies the multitude of conflicts that have been part of its genesis.

A study carried out by CEDR in 2006 revealed that approximately 80 per cent of the costs associated with the poor handling of conflict are attributable to lost productivity, damaged relationships and tarnished reputations (with the remaining 20 per cent relating to legal fees).

Distraction costs are a key area of concern: members of the project team who are occupied with resolving disputes will not be fully available for new projects, having instead to prepare for a trial or arbitration and brief lawyers or experts about the project and the dispute. CEDR's research showed that a typical £1 million value dispute takes up over three years of line managers' time in trying to sort it out: a cost of conflict which far outweighs the legal and other professional fees involved.

Unresolved disputes result in job stress, and the emotional cost can be substantial. People can become so emotionally involved in the dispute that they have problems engaging with those who would be part of its resolution and will find it hard to look at the dispute from a perspective outside their own perception of the relationships between the parties; for a project manager, this can become a real deterrent. Relationships start to deteriorate; the project team sees that and knows there is a problem. Even if the dispute is dealt with, there is the possibility of the hangover of the dispute transferring to another project.

A study of 100 in-house lawyers and managers in public and private sector organisations commissioned by law firm Nabarro and published in July 2007 identified that, although risk-management policies were in place in the majority of the organisations, there were mixed opinions about their effectiveness. Only 12 per cent had risk policies that covered dispute resolution in detail, and many had no policy at all. Risk policies were often not updated in light of lessons learnt from disputes, and only 38 per cent had programmes to educate staff on dispute prevention. Poor communication, followed by 'failure to deliver', were cited as the two top causes of disputes. For public sector organisations the figures were 20 per cent higher in each case.

With work relationships, job progress, job satisfaction and profitability at risk, preventing disputes during the course of a project is preferable to resolution at a later time. The parties need to be proactive in resolving conflicts before their positions become hardened.

Managing the risk of disputes

Disputes are perhaps the last thing that contracting parties want to think about after involving themselves in a lengthy and expensive bidding and negotiation process.

While it is easy to point to disputes arising out of any number of procurement, design and operational management activities, all these areas of activity have substantial human variables. Project teams must increasingly take into account different cultures and the possibility that members of the project team will come with different problem resolution philosophies. There may be great inequality among project team members in their ability to deal with problems and disputes and it is often easy for members of the project team to fall back on adversarial behaviours, turning the contract into an arena for combat.

In addition, certain types of complex projects, or projects of a prototype nature involving new or specialised technologies which involve multicontracting regimes, bring more interfaces and specialised teams to manage.

Projects that are politically sensitive or subject to possible government intervention demand even more attention to dispute risk management. Project finance is often used to fund investments in higher-risk developing countries, particularly for large infrastructure and natural resource extraction projects. Often these investments are linked to violent conflict at local and national levels associated with economic underdevelopment and natural resource dependence. Not only do project financiers have to be concerned about managing their exposure to conflict-related risks, but there are also tighter requirements on banks and the project management team to have in place efficient risk-management processes at operational level.

A clear approach to dispute resolution is particularly needed in long-term contracts since the parties' relationships will continue both throughout and after the dispute. A successful resolution of the issues will often involve both the resolution of the issues and a reconsideration of, or possibly a variation to, the contract to prevent future disputes.

Where a collaborative contracting approach is being adopted, conflict management must be integral to it. A collaborative relationship takes time to become established and to avoid complacency it must be managed continuously. It requires energy and drive to make it happen, which may not always come from within the project team.

Despite the fact that communication and relationship problems are cited in research as the most common reason for disputes, many organisations still ignore the importance of managing relationships within the project team as part of a dispute prevention function.

"many organisations still ignore the importance of managing relationships"

Partnering

The trick in construction projects is to establish and maintain stable relationships. This is no revelation, having been transformed into the concept of partnering.

Partnering is more to do with increasing the effectiveness of communication than it is to do with risk sharing. At its heart lies a commitment by executive managers to adopt a collaborative approach to a project. The approach is used to arrive at business objectives by looking to optimise each of the partner organisations' resources. One of the aims of partnering, therefore, is to increase productivity and so generate more successful outcomes to contract performance.

A written document is not necessary for partnering to be effective. However, it is generally the case that partnering begins with setting out joint objectives in writing after the contract is signed. This is generally thought to be the most effective approach, but is not a fixed feature of partnering.

Some form of partnering charter or agreement is the usual end product of a partnering workshop. This sets out the ground rules for how everybody will work together. However, the partnering charter, unlike the main contract, is not usually binding. Including a requirement for a partnering workshop in contract documents is not, therefore, a guarantee of improved productivity. Usually, it is necessary to provide training in working as a partnering team if a contract partnering agreement is to be adopted successfully. The partnering charter, therefore, introduces a collective responsibility that may seem to be at odds with the main contract, in which the individual responsibilities of the parties are defined. This anomaly was addressed in the first standard form of partnering contract, the Project Partnering Contract 2000 (PPC 2000), published by the Association of Consultant Architects in June 2000. PPC 2000 integrates the entire project team under a single multiparty contract and covers the duration of the procurement process. This avoids the need for several biparty professional appointments separated from the building contract and/or partnering agreement and removes the temptation for parties to hide behind unconnected biparty agreements.

The two main options for partnering are, therefore, as follows:

- *Traditional contract and partnering charter* – although the partnering charter in itself has no legality, its terms could be taken into account in determining whether the parties had adopted attitudes and conduct in accordance with its spirit and intention.

• *Partnering contracts* – the partnering contract provides both incentives and penalties to encourage exceptional performance. Additionally, it establishes performance measurement criteria to be used during the contract period. Without measurement criteria it is difficult to assess whether performance is improving. This is particularly important for strategic partnering arrangements involving a series of repeat projects and where the familiarity of the relationship could lead to a slacking-off in performance. There are two main alternative frameworks for partnering contracts:

  – *Client centred* – the client engages all individual members of the design team, the project manager and the contractor. The client is open to claims from the contractor if a member of the design team is late in providing information to the contractor.
  – *Contractor centred* – the client engages a single contractor who is responsible for engaging all members of the design team, including specialist subcontractors. The contractor is responsible for coordinating the work of everyone involved on the project. Liability for inadequate performance of any member of the design team or specialist subcontractors lies with the contractor.

Contracts promoting principles of collaborative working

A contract in itself neither makes relationships work nor provides a quick fix for building or rebuilding relationships. Indeed, the length and complexity of contracts, which can now run into thousands of pages, leaves more scope for differences in interpretation to emerge. A so-called 'suitable' contract cannot be relied upon in its entirety to reduce the impact of negative conflict. Nevertheless, certain contracts, such as the New Engineering Contract 3rd edition (NEC3), the Joint Contracts Tribunal Constructing Excellence Contract (JCT/Ce), and the Association of Consultant Architects Project Partnering Contract 2000 (PPC 2000) and Term Partnering Contract 2005 (TPC 2005) do place emphasis on promoting collaborative and integrated working through regulating the relationships in a project. They adopt different structures for doing so.

With PPC 2000, parties agree to partner and contract as a single entity to achieve project and commercial interests. It has its own subcontract for subcontractors who are not partners. Members of the project team owe a duty of care to each other. However, the level of duty will differ between the individual parties involved and it may be extremely difficult to assess the full extent of liability a party is assuming under the contract. This differs from JCT/Ce, which has a series of bilateral contracts within the multiparty document. Each bilateral contract establishes a duty from one party to another.

NEC3 includes Option X12, a partnering charter that can be used for some or all parties. It creates a multiparty partnering team where the parties cooperate to achieve each other's project interests. They contract separately and partner together. The thrust behind the development of the NEC3 suite of contracts, which is endorsed by the Office of Government Commerce for public sector construction procurement, was to prompt good management practice and to initiate collaborative working. The guidance note to NEC3 says that key to its successful use is 'users adopting the desired cultural transition': a transition which involves changing from a hindsight-based decision-making and management approach to a forward-looking one encompassing collaborative relationships. That cultural transition is one that may not come easily to many organisations.

Another difference between the contracts is that PPC 2000 and NEC contracts require the parties to establish core groups to make key decisions whereas the JCT/Ce contract does not.

There has been much debate about the extent to which the partnering process affects the rights and obligations of the parties under a contract and whether in common-law jurisdictions there exists an implied duty to perform a contract in good faith. This debate was prompted by the fact that partnering has been borrowed from the USA, whose legal system recognises the doctrine of good faith in contracting.

From this has emerged one key criticism of all partnering arrangements, which is that the obligations are vague. For example, PPC 2000 requires the project team to 'work together and individually in the spirit of trust, fairness and mutual co-operation'. What does that really mean?

Non-escalation mechanisms and mediation

Non-escalation mechanisms cover tiered dispute resolution clauses, including ad hoc or mandatory mediation within contracts, the use of dispute boards and project mediation.

All these mechanisms prompt considerations at procurement stage regarding:

- whether to use an ad hoc or institutional procedure
- whether the procedure is single-stage or multistage
- the timescales involved
- whether the procedure covers all or certain types of dispute
- the cost – which would also include setting financial thresholds, where possible, to reduce the risk of the cost of resolution exceeding the value of the dispute.

One potential difficulty with tiered dispute resolution provisions is the length of time it can take to work through the various steps involved. Escalating negotiation clauses often involve second or possibly third stages, which can take weeks, or longer, to comply with. Where the parties end up in a dispute, they may have been negotiating the issue for some time before one party triggers the dispute resolution clause's formal process. On the other hand, the opportunity to resolve disputes at operational level may be lost if all disputes have to be elevated to senior executive level. (It is also questionable how effective a formal first stage of senior executive discussions is in practice.)

Next, where is mediation located on the problem resolution ladder? Can it only be used at one stage of the procedure?

If mediation is available at any time it means there is a greater chance for productive discussions because the parties are actually ready to engage in mediation. A compulsory mediation stage close to the outset of a dispute may not give a party enough time to have a genuine understanding of either its own factual and legal positions or those of the other party.

"If mediation is available at any time there is a greater chance for productive discussions"

Another consideration relates to the situation where one party seeks delay by arguing that the parties have not yet engaged in 'amicable' or 'good faith' negotiations, as referred to in the dispute resolution provisions. Asking the parties to engage in amicable settlement discussions first and then, if unsuccessful, moving to a next stage says nothing about what the parties are actually meant to do and for how long.

If mandatory negotiation or mediation is included, it is wise to consider short time limits before the parties can move on to the next stage. If the negotiation is going well then the parties can always agree to extend the time period. The point is that if one party does not play ball, it cannot use failure to comply to stop the other party from moving to the next dispute resolution stage. Phrases such as 'reasonable endeavours' or 'good faith' are not always helpful; they can be used as a vehicle for delay or as an attempt to short-circuit the negotiation process.

Enforcement of ADR clauses

Generally, parties comply voluntarily with ADR clauses, but what happens where one party fails to do so?

The enforceability of ADR clauses was dealt with by the judgment in the case of *Cable & Wireless plc v. IBM UK Ltd* (2002) in respect of an escalating dispute resolution procedure which provided for negotiation between senior executives, then mediation and, finally, litigation. Following unsuccessful negotiation, Cable & Wireless refused mediation and IBM started proceedings. Cable & Wireless then asked for the Commercial Court to give a declaration that the mediation clause was no more enforceable than an agreement to negotiate. The Court, however, thought differently. The mediation clause was enforceable principally on the ground that the contract provided for a specific procedure to be used in the dispute resolution hierarchy, covering detailed aspects of the procedure and termination. The mediation clause therefore anticipated a minimum level of participation by the parties. It went much further than simply stating that the parties would attempt to negotiate in good faith, giving 'engagements of sufficient certainty' for a court to determine compliance with a mediation provision.

This judgment leaves no doubt as to the enforceability of clauses compelling parties to negotiate or mediate prior to litigation or arbitration. It also reinforced the point that reference to a known and accepted model mediation procedure will give greater weight to a mediation clause. The parties can always include a provision that allows for proceedings to be commenced at the same time, and alongside, ADR to provide protective relief, to protect their rights, or generally to show the seriousness with which they take an issue.

PFI contracts

For PFI contracts, section 28 of HM Treasury's *Standardisation of PFI Contracts* (SoPC4) (as published in March 2007) suggests a three-stage dispute resolution process, encompassing direct negotiation between the authority and the contractor, expert determination and, ultimately, arbitration or the courts if either party is dissatisfied with the expert's decision. SoPC4 also says 'it may be appropriate in certain circumstances to substitute other forms of Alternative Dispute Resolution' for the expert determination stage, and a footnote identifies mediation, conciliation and neutral evaluation as possible alternatives. Attention is also drawn to the disparity between the dispute resolution procedure in the project agreement and that imposed by the Housing Grants, Construction and Regeneration Act 1996 on a subcontract which, within the meaning of the act, is a 'construction contract'. Although the parties may be willing to use different forms of ADR at project agreement level, there will be a disparity between the project agreement and the subcontract dispute resolution process, which gives a right for either party to refer a dispute to adjudication at any time.

Arbitration or litigation as the last resort?

There are a number of key factors to consider in choosing arbitration or litigation as the last resort to settle the dispute:

- *Confidentiality* – unlike a court hearing, which is open to the public, arbitration is held in private and all matters dealt with under the arbitration are confidential unless the parties agree otherwise.
- *Choice of decision-maker* – unlike litigation, in which the parties have no say in the choice of the judge, in arbitration the parties can choose an arbitrator (or arbitrators) with specific technical or legal expertise relevant to the subject matter of the case. In addition, once appointed, the arbitrator will manage the case for its duration; in litigation proceedings a number of different judges may hear interim applications.
- *Control of process* – the Arbitration Act 1996 (the Act) sets out a number of powers that arbitrators are free to adopt unless the parties agree otherwise. Under section 33 of the Act arbitrators must 'adopt procedures suitable to the circumstances of the particular case, avoiding unnecessary delay or expense', and section 34 of the Act also sets out examples of procedural matters that the arbitrators can exercise. However, the parties can choose the procedure best suited to the nature of their case, and the procedure that the parties choose cannot be overruled by the arbitrator. The Act also specifies powers that the arbitrator cannot exercise unless expressly agreed by the parties. Among others, this includes the power to direct joinder and

the consolidation of related proceedings to enable them to be dealt with simultaneously by the arbitrator. This is significant in the context of PFI agreements.

- *Appeals against decisions* – under the Act the ability to appeal to the High Court against an arbitration award is limited to circumstances where:
  - a party believes that the arbitrator had no jurisdiction to hear the case
  - there was serious irregularity in the conduct of the arbitration, such as the arbitrator acting outside his or her powers
  - a party wishes to appeal on a point of law (but only allowable in limited circumstances).

  Parties can agree to exclude the right to appeal from their arbitration agreement or clause.
- *Arbitration costs and duration* – where a dispute involves complex issues, extensive documentation, large numbers of witnesses and/or technical issues requiring a number of expert witnesses, then arbitration may be more expensive and more time-consuming than litigation in the courts. Whereas a court judge is free to the parties, each arbitrator is paid a fee; this may become expensive when three arbitrators are involved. Parties must also pay for the arbitration venue. Because there is no administrative system to control the availability of arbitrators, it may prove very difficult with a three-person arbitration panel to book hearing times when all the arbitrators can attend.

Dispute boards

Where a contract provides for a dispute board it will be as part of a tiered dispute resolution clause. A clause might provide for a dispute board to operate throughout the project, for some technical disputes or disputes with financial thresholds to be referable, in certain circumstances, to senior executives and/or independent experts, mediation and, finally, arbitration or court.

A dispute board creates an environment in which the parties are encouraged not to exaggerate any representations that they may make to each other because they will know that at some point the board members may be asked to intervene. The same board reviews all project disputes, therefore the parties become accustomed to how the board will react and will take that into consideration when negotiating with each other. In that way claims are avoided and many disputes are likely to settle before being put to the board. The regular on-site presence of the dispute board members is likely to encourage cooperative behaviour among the parties; neither party will want to be seen as the cause of a dispute in front of the dispute board members, particularly as the same people will be dealing with all disputes.

The effect of the dispute board has also been explained as the development of 'an unexpected dynamic'; site staff and operational managers, who work with each other every day, see the dispute board members as intruders who must be sided against to prevent them interfering with the site's private business. Parties, therefore, quickly come to a compromise.

There are three main types of dispute board:

* *Dispute Review Board* (DRB) – commonplace on domestic US construction projects, DRBs give a non-binding recommendation. In the majority of cases, these recommendations are accepted; the Dispute Review Board Foundation records that 97 per cent of disputes referred to DRBs are resolved without going to court or arbitration.
  A DRB established under a contract between employer and main contractor can be empowered to hear disputes arising at lower levels of the contracting hierarchy. Obviously, such arrangements need to be structured at the time the subcontractors are engaged.
* *Dispute Adjudication Board* (DAB) – under the rules of the International Federation of Consulting Engineers (FIDIC) the DAB is appointed as a consequence of a FIDIC contract between an employer and a contractor. The DAB can only deal with disputes between that employer and the contractor that arise under, or in connection with, that contract. If the contractor or the employer has a dispute with the engineer, or with some other agency, then the DAB does not have the jurisdiction to consider that dispute. However, if the engineer is acting on behalf of the employer, then the employer will be responsible for the engineer's actions. The dispute is then between the contractor and employer and can, therefore, be considered by the DAB. Similarly, a dispute between the contractor and a subcontractor cannot be considered by the DAB. However, many subcontractor disputes are also disputes between the contractor and the employer.
  Members of the DAB must act in a judicial capacity because the DAB is giving a decision (albeit an interim one) which interprets the rights and obligations of the parties to a contract. So, the DAB must not only consider the facts but also the applicable law and must follow the rules of natural justice. This means that the DAB cannot act as a mediator. The DAB, unlike a mediator,

cannot meet privately with each party in order to discuss information and matters which one party does not want the other party to know. It would risk basing its decision on information which had not been disclosed to the other party.

- *Dispute Management Board* (DMB) – the DMB is an independent advisory board which is attached to the project management team. It observes the early stages of the team's work and subsequently pays regular updating visits during the life of the project.

  The DMB will comprise a number of different specialists or experts, and one or more of its members will often adopt the role of a conciliator, advising the project team on the best way to address any problems identified by the DMB as a whole. Alternatively, it may adopt the role of a mediator, facilitating discussions between members of the project team aimed at producing a dispute settlement agreement.

When projects involve multicontracting regimes or a series of projects on a substantial construction programme it may be difficult to maintain a number of dispute boards, and there may be issues regarding continuity and general oversight of the programme as a whole. In these circumstances it may be appropriate to have a single dispute board in place for all projects throughout the construction programme. The advantage of this arrangement is that the dispute board will be in a position to look at the dispute resolution landscape over the entire construction programme. However, the convening and administration of the dispute board will require more effort.

Project mediation

While dispute boards are successful in dealing with legal and contractual issues, interteam and intrateam problems may be less well catered for. This also reflects the point that traditional risk management approaches rely mainly on the implementation of a methodology that focuses on technical aspects and which usually leaves out ways of dealing with communication and relationship issues in projects.

Project mediation, like dispute boards, is a non-escalation mechanism set up at the start of a contract. However, the level of interaction of the project mediator and the dispute board member with the project team is different. The project mediator (or mediators) has a team-building role, bringing conflict resolution and communication expertise as well as technical and contractual expertise. The value of the communication role should not be underestimated.

In the context of information flow between the owner and the project manager, research has shown that there is a substantial difference between low- and high-performing projects in terms of the owner's desire for communication and its perception of project performance. On high-performing projects, the owner had a much greater desire for communication, but also a lower perception of project performance than that held by the project manager. Conversely, on low-performing projects, the owner had less desire for communication, but a higher perception of project performance than that held by the project manager.

Research has also shown that delays and disruptions have a much greater impact on cost overruns than project managers intuitively expect, and that many technically focused project managers confuse fast exchange of information with effective communication.

Typically, project team members have access to one or two project mediators, who visit the site on a regular basis to discuss progress and to identify with the parties any actual or potential communication or technical problems. Visits will normally coincide with the regular project or site meetings. The project mediators may have discussions with the contractor, owner or any member of the project team, including consultants, subcontractors and specialist suppliers, collectively referred to as 'key suppliers'. The key suppliers are joined into the project mediation agreement between the owner and the contractor, referred to as the 'core parties'.

Before the project starts, the project mediators arrange a partnering workshop attended by all project decision-makers. The project mediators also receive core documentation to review during the course of the works and they may be contacted at any time to discuss project concerns and to seek guidance. If required, the parties may enter into a formal mediation conducted by the project mediators.

Costs of dispute boards and project mediation

Ad hoc panels can also be established at the time a dispute arises. However, there are problems with this approach. The most obvious is that the potential for preventing disputes has already been lost. Also, although it may appear that the parties will save on costs, they will ultimately incur additional costs because of the extra time required to establish the panel in a time of conflict and because the bulk of disputes will be decided by the panel only after project completion.

Costs very much depend on the individual project. Generally, though, the costs of dispute boards remain below 2 per cent of the contract value. This needs to be compared with the costs of arbitration, which normally exceed 5 per cent of the contract value. Also, the costs of a dispute board are offset by the lower bid prices that are known to result when contractors prepare tenders, particularly when working overseas.

The cost of project mediation will be less than using a dispute board because it will not be necessary to establish and maintain a three-person board. While it is true that FIDIC and the World Bank encourage one-person dispute boards for smaller projects, project mediation adds a greater degree of flexibility in terms of process and level of involvement. Even though it can be adopted after the contract has started, the use of project mediation, like dispute boards, should not be seen as a distress purchase. The potential benefits of project mediation will be lost if it is not integrated as part of a business or project strategy.

```
┌─────────────────────── SUMMARY ───────────────────────┐
```

Dispute prevention and conflict management – non-escalation mechanisms and mediation

Non-escalation mechanisms need to address the following questions:

Procedure

- Will the non-escalation mechanism refer to an existing set of procedural rules or will it have its own rules?

Single-step or multistep

- In the event of a problem or dispute, is mediation the first step or is it preceded by direct negotiations?
- Is mediation to take place before or during arbitration or litigation or can it take place at any time? While it is not possible to sidestep the jurisdiction of the courts, it will stay proceedings to allow parties to fulfil their agreement to mediate.

A trigger for the process

- Is the process initiated by a formal notice of dispute, letter from senior manager or agreement by executive group?

Timescales

- Particularly if mandatory negotiation or mediation is to be included, what time limits will be specified before the parties can move to the next sage?

Decision-makers

- Will the non-escalation mechanism identify decision-makers (with full authority) from each party or will it make a general reference to decision-makers, leaving the parties to decide at the relevant time which individual will be the decision-maker?

Types of dispute covered

- Will the procedure apply to all disputes or only to certain types?

Financial thresholds

- Can thresholds be set to make sure that the cost of resolution does not exceed the value of the claim or dispute?

┌─────────── **. . . AND FINALLY** ───────────┐

This guide started with an example of how the inadequate management of a dispute led to the legal costs on a domestic project becoming disproportionate to the value of the claim. If that has not persuaded you of the value of mediation, look at what happened on a high-profile commercial project: the Wembley Stadium.

Multiplex Constructions (UK) Ltd (Multiplex), the main contractor, and Cleveland Bridge UK Ltd (Cleveland), the steelwork subcontractor, had a tense relationship which came to an acrimonious end in August 2004.

Multiplex made a claim for damages arising out of alleged defects and repudiation of contract, and Cleveland cross-claimed for sums due for work done and materials supplied. The claim and the cross-claim were subsequently consolidated into a single action at the end of 2004.

At a case management conference on 5 December 2005, the judge discussed with leading counsel how the disputes might most economically be resolved. Nine preliminary issues were identified (later increased to 11), the answers to which would provide a good platform for the parties to resolve their differences.

In his judgment of the preliminary issues in 2006, the judge told the parties that 'with the assistance of this court's decision on the [preliminary issues], it may now be possible for both parties to arrive at an overall settlement of their disputes, either through negotiation or else with the help of a mediator, who is unconnected with this court'. Although the court would determine any remaining issues that the parties wanted to litigate, it was encouraging the parties to enter into a sensible commercial settlement.

Regardless, and despite an unsuccessful mediation along the way, the parties served pleadings, witness statements and evidence in readiness for the trial scheduled to start in March 2008. The litigation 'red button' had not only been pressed, but, as the judge commented: 'Whilst the parties were battling out the 11 preliminary issues at all levels, their enthusiasm for the main fray never wavered. All thoughts of reaching a sensible settlement after resolution of the preliminary issues ... were seemingly jettisoned ... both parties have brushed aside repeated judicial observations on the wisdom of settling this particular litigation'.

So, after a three-month trial, judgment was made in favour of Multiplex in the sum of £6.15 million in respect of overpayments made by Multiplex to Cleveland, damages for breach of contract and interest. The costs up to the preliminary issues hearing were £8 million. The costs after the preliminary issues hearing were £14 million, including a £1 million bill for photocopying!

Appendix A
The courts' attitudes on refusals to mediate

There have been many decisions that demonstrate the willingness of the courts to take into account the behaviour of the parties before trial, penalising those who have unreasonably refused to attempt mediation or other forms of ADR. Some notable cases include the following:

- *Dyson & Fields v. Leeds City Council* [1999] WL 1142459

  The Court of Appeal set out the likely consequences for parties who are seen to have acted unreasonably by failing to use ADR. The court made it clear that this was a case in which it expected mediation to have been tried before the rehearing it had ordered. It emphasised that it had powers to take a strong line with any party reluctant to engage in mediation by imposing eventual orders for indemnity costs or ordering that a higher rate of interest be paid on any damages awarded.

- *Paul Thomas Construction Ltd v. Damian Hyland and Jackie Power* (2000) TCC

  At a hearing in which applications by the claimant had been dismissed, the judge required justification of the conduct of the claimant in issuing proceedings. At a further adjourned hearing the judge held that the claimant had adopted a heavy-handed approach, which was very much at odds with the Technology and Construction Court ethos that ran through the Civil Procedure Rules. The judge observed that it had been wholly unnecessary to start the litigation and that ADR could, and should, have been explored. That could have included direct discussions not involving a third party. The judge also held that indemnity costs were warranted.

• Lord Chancellor's Department (23 March 2001)

The Government makes a formal pledge that: 'Government departments and agencies make these commitments on the resolution of disputes involving them. Alternative Dispute Resolution will be considered and used in all suitable cases wherever the other party accepts it.' Departments also undertook to provide appropriate clauses on the use of ADR in their standard procurement contracts.

• *Cowl v. Plymouth City Council*, The Times, 8 January 2002

The Lord Chief Justice, Lord Woolf, reminded those engaged in public law cases that litigation should be the last resort. He suggested that the court might, on its own initiative, fix a hearing at which the parties could be required to explain what they had done to resolve a dispute without resort to the courts.

• *Dunnett v. Railtrack* [2002] All ER 850

The first example of a successful litigant winning at trial (including an appeal) but losing the subsequent costs award because of an unreasonable refusal to follow the court's suggestion to attempt mediation. In the judgment, parties were warned that if they 'turn down out of hand the chance of ADR, when suggested by the court … they may have to face uncomfortable costs consequences'.

• *Leicester Circuits Limited v. Coates Brothers plc* [2003] EWCA Civ 333

The Court of Appeal penalised a successful appellant in relation to its costs of the trial in a lower court because it withdrew from a mediation the day before it was due to take place. The defendant, which withdrew from mediation, lost at trial but succeeded on appeal. Its costs in the lower court were awarded in its favour up to the time that the mediation was agreed, but thereafter, including the trial, each party had to bear its own costs. The court commented that 'it hardly lies in the mouths of those who agreed to mediation to assert that there was no realistic prospect of success'.

- *Royal Bank of Canada Trust Corporation Ltd v. Secretary of State for Defence* [2003] EWHC 1479

This case centred on a point of law concerning the interpretation of a break clause in a lease. The claimant had expressed its willingness to resolve the matter by ADR but the suggestion of mediation was rejected by the defendant, on the basis that the dispute:

- turned on a point of law – requiring a 'black and white' answer
- involved commercial parties, not individuals
- did not involve circumstances where emotions were running high or played a significant part in the conflict between the parties.

On the point of law, the Secretary of State for Defence ('the Department') was successful. However, in relation to costs, the claimant drew the court's attention to the Government's 'ADR pledge'.

The judge severely penalised the Department for refusing to mediate. He noted the reasons for refusal as 'surprising' and stated that they did not make the matter unsuitable for mediation. The judge declined to award any costs to the Department, effectively removing the financial gain obtained through the successful action.

- *Corenso (UK) Ltd v. Burnden Group plc* [2003] EWHC 1805

This action settled following a Part 36 offer. The defendant had proposed mediation but the court refused to grant costs relief on that basis. Although the court considered that a failure to engage in mediation can have adverse cost consequences for a successful party, it did not consider that this conclusion was inevitable. The court emphasised that the requirement under the Civil Procedure Rules is to engage in ADR, not necessarily mediation. In this case there had been a number of attempts at settlement and the court concluded that: 'So long as parties are showing a genuine and constructive willingness to resolve the issues between them, it does not seem... that a party will automatically be penalised because that party has not gone along with a particular form of ADR proposed by the other side'.

- *Hurst v. Leeming* [2003] 1 Lloyd's Rep 379

The court declined the unsuccessful claimant's request that costs sanctions be imposed on the defendant for rejecting offers to mediate both before and after proceedings had been issued. Because of the obsessive attitude of the claimant, the court considered it was reasonable for the defendant to refuse mediation. Like the Dunnett case, the judgment placed a burden on the successful party to show that it was reasonable to have refused mediation.

- *Shirayama Shokusan v. Danovo Ltd* [2003] EWHC 3006 (Ch)

Despite resistance from the claimant, the court granted an order for mediation, considering that the case management powers in the Civil Procedure Rules entitled it to order mediation even against the wishes of a party. As the case involved a dispute over a 20-year subunder lease, the court took the view that, with the likely prospect of a long-term relationship, much would be gained if mediation succeeded.

- *Halsey v. Milton Keynes General NHS Trust and Steel v. Joy and Halliday* [2004] EWCA 576

The Court of Appeal considered the question of costs where one party refuses to mediate but wins at trial. It concluded that the parties had acted reasonably and, therefore, the refusal to mediate did not threaten the successful defendant's entitlement to its costs. The judgment also held that it was inappropriate for the courts to compel unwilling parties, including public authorities, to submit a dispute to ADR. However, it gave broad support for the use of mediation and stated that it is suitable in many disputes and confirmed the role of the courts to actively encourage ADR.

- *Couwenberg v. Valkova* [2004] EWCA Civ 676

This case involved allegations of fraud and alleged forgery in relation to letters asserting proper attestation of a will. The claimant sought permission to appeal on the basis of fresh evidence that might show that a fraud had been perpetrated in relation to the will.

In granting permission to appeal, the Court of Appeal considered that mediation would be appropriate, contrary to the observations in the Halsey case that mediation is not appropriate in cases involving fraud allegations.

- *Reed Executive v. Reed Business Information* [2004] EWCA Civ 887

  The claimant sought an order for costs claiming that, even though they had lost on appeal, the defendant had refused to engage in mediation. The defendant argued that this issue could not be decided without reference to certain 'without prejudice' correspondence, which is inadmissible.

  The Court of Appeal decided that a court can neither order disclosure of 'without prejudice' correspondence against the wishes of one of the parties when deciding the issue of costs for refusing to engage in ADR, nor can it draw an adverse inference against the party who refuses the disclosure.

  Any party wishing to disclose correspondence to the court on the issue of costs should ensure that the offer to mediate is made in open correspondence or in correspondence marked 'without prejudice save as to costs'.

  On the documents available, the court concluded that the defendant had not unreasonably refused to mediate on account that the parties had already incurred substantial legal costs prior to the mediation proposal, and that the defendant had reasonable belief in its prospects of success on appeal.

- *Burchell v. Bullard* [2005] EWCA Civ 358

  Before starting proceedings the claimant (a small builder) suggested mediation to the owners to resolve a claim for £18,000. The owners' building surveyor said that mediation was not suitable because of the complex technical issues involved. The refusal to mediate took place before May 2001, when the courts' approach to cost penalties on parties refusing to mediate had not yet been established. Lord Justice Ward in the Court of Appeal did not penalise the building owners; however, his judgment made clear that:

  - interparty offers to mediate, whether made before proceedings or before appeal, must be taken seriously and that the court's recommendation to mediate is not needed to give rise to the possibility of cost sanctions
  - a party showing willingness to engage flexibly in mediation may well discharge the burden of proving that mediation had a reasonable prospect of success
  - those who ignore an ADR proposal at the pre-issue meeting as given in the Construction Pre-Action Protocol 'can expect little sympathy if they blithely battle on regardless of the alternatives'

- the fact that a professional advisor advises his or her client to decline mediation will not protect that client from cost sanctions if mediation ought reasonably to have been attempted.

- *P4 Ltd v. Unite Integrated Solutions plc* [2006] EWHC TCC 2924

The Technology and Construction Court considered the effect of the defendant's refusal to mediate and failure to provide information before the start of proceedings. The judge held that the defendant was not entitled to costs to which it was otherwise entitled, and also commented that 'I do not consider that letters from solicitors which make offers can be a proper substitute for the process of ADR which involves clients engaging with each other and a third party such as a mediator to resolve a dispute'.

Appendix B
Model settlement agreement and Tomlin order

Date

Parties

_____ ("Party A")

[Address]^1 _____

_____ ("Party B")

[Address]^2 _____

[_____ ("Party C") etc.]
(jointly "the Parties")

[Background]

The Parties have agreed to settle "the Dispute" which:

- is being litigated/arbitrated [court/arbitration reference] ("the Action")^4
- has been the subject of a CEDR Solve mediation today ("the Mediation")

Terms

It is agreed as follows:

   1 [A will deliver .... to B at .... by not later than 4 o'clock on 25 December.....]^5

2 [B will pay £......... to A by not later than 4 o'clock on 25 December.....
   by direct bank transfer to .... bank sort code .... account
   number ....]

3 [Add additional terms as required]

4a The Action will be stayed and the parties will consent to an order in the terms
    of the attached Tomlin Order precedent [see attachment].

OR

4b The Action will be dismissed with no order as to costs.

5 This Agreement is in full and final settlement of any causes of action what-
   soever which the Parties [and any subsidiaries .... of the Parties] have
   against each other.

6 This agreement supersedes all previous agreements between the parties [in
   respect of matters the subject of the Mediation].[6]

7 If any dispute arises out of this Agreement, the Parties will attempt to settle it
   by mediation[7] before resorting to any other means of dispute resolution. To
   institute any such mediation a party must give notice to the mediator of the
   Mediation. Insofar as possible the terms of the Mediation Agreement will
   apply to any such further mediation. If no legally binding settlement of
   this dispute is reached within [28] days from the date of the notice to the
   Mediator, either party may [institute court proceedings / refer the dispute
   to arbitration under the rules of......].

8 The Parties will keep confidential and not use for any collateral or ulterior
   purpose the terms of this Agreement [except insofar as is necessary to
   implement and enforce any of its terms].

9 This Agreement shall be governed by, construed and take effect in
   accordance with [English] law. The courts of [England] shall have exclusive
   jurisdiction to settle any claim, dispute or matter of difference which may
   arise out of, or in connection with this agreement.[8]

Signed

for and on behalf of[9]

_____

or and on behalf of[10]

_____

Note: This Model Agreement and attached precedent order is for guidance only. Any agreement based on it will need to be adapted to the particular circumstances and legal requirements of the settlement to which it relates. Wherever possible any such agreement should be drafted/approved by each party's lawyer. Although the mediator is likely to be involved in helping the parties to draft acceptable terms, the mediator is not responsible for the drafting of the agreement and does not need to be a party to it. [See also provisions of mediation agreement which, if it is based on the CEDR Model Mediation Agreement, will deal with mediator liability, confidentially etc. and should not need to be repeated in this agreement.]

Attachment to Model Settlement Agreement

Tomlin Order Precedent

[Action heading]

UPON hearing . . . . .

By consent

IT IS ORDERED that all further proceedings in this case be stayed upon the terms set out in the Settlement Agreement between Parties dated . . . . ., an original of which is held by each of the Parties' solicitors [OR CEDR Solve/the Mediator] except for the purpose of enforcing the terms of that Agreement as set out below.

AND IT IS FURTHER ORDERED that either Party/any of the Parties may apply to the court to enforce the terms of the said Agreement [or to claim for breach of it] without the need to commence new proceedings.

AND IT IS FURTHER ORDERED that [each Party bear its own costs].

WE CONSENT to an order in these terms

_____ [Black & White], Claimant's Solicitors

_____ [Red & Green], Defendant's Solicitors

_____

(Reproduced with the permission of CEDR)

1 Not strictly necessary
2 Not strictly necessary
3 Not strictly necessary but may be useful for setting up definitions
4 Omit this wording and paragraph 4 if there are no court proceedings
5 Be as specific as possible, for example, how, by when, etc.
6 Only necessary if there have been previous agreements
7 Alternatively, negotiation at Chief Executive level, followed by mediation if negotiations do not result in settlement within a specified time
8 Usually not necessary where parties are located in same country and subject matter of agreement relates to one country
9 Not necessary where the party signing is an individual
10 Not necessary where the party signing is an individual

Appendix C
Websites for further ADR-related information

General

Academy of Experts	www.academy-experts.org
Adjudication Society	www.adjudication.org
ADR Group	www.adrgroup.co.uk
Centre for Effective Dispute Resolution	www.cedr.com
Chartered Institute of Building	www.ciob.org.uk
Civil Mediation Council	www.civilmediation.org
Construction and Conciliation Group	www.ccgroup.org.uk
Construction Industry Council	www.cic.org.uk
Core Solutions Group Ltd	www.core-solutions.com
Dispute Board Federation	www.dbfederation.org
Dispute Resolution Board Foundation	www.drb.org
IDRS Ltd	www.idrs.ltd.uk
Institution of Civil Engineers	www.ice.org
International Federation of Consulting Engineers	www.fidic.org
Law Society	www.lawsociety.org.uk
London Court of International Arbitration	www.lcia-arbitration.com
Royal Institute of British Architects	www.architecture.com
Royal Institution of Chartered Surveyors	www.rics.org
Society of Construction Law	www.scl.org.uk
Technology and Construction Bar Association	www.tecbar.org
Technology and Construction Solicitors Association	www.tecsa.org.uk

Contracts

NEC	www.neccontract.com
PPC2000 and TPC2005	www.ppc2000.co.uk
JCT/Ce	www.jctltd.co.uk

Government departments/agencies: advisory

Office of Government Commerce	www.ogc.gov.uk
Pre-Action Protocol for Construction and Engineering Disputes	www.justice.gov.uk/civil/procrules_fin/contents/protocols/prot_ced.htm
Standardisation of PFI Contracts Version 4	www.hm-treasury.gov.uk

References

Publications

Centre for Effective Dispute Resolution (CEDR) (2008). *CEDR Solve Rules for Construction Adjudication.* CEDR.

CEDR (2006). *Conflict is costing business £33 billion every year.* CEDR; online at www.cedr.com/index.php?location=/news/archive/20060526_232.htm

Egan, Sir John (1998). *Rethinking Construction.* DETR.

Fisher R. and Ury W. (1981). *Getting to Yes.* Business Books.

HM Treasury (2007). *Standardisation of PFI Contracts* (SoPC4). HM Treasury.

Latham, Sir Michael (1994). *Constructing the Team.* HMSO.

Nabarro (2007). *Controlling conflict – The management and avoidance of disputes.* Nabarro; online at www.nabarro.com/downloads/controlling%conflict.pdf

National Audit Office (2001), *Modernising Construction.* The Stationery Office.

Contracts

JCT – Constructing Excellence Contract (JCT/Ce). Joint Contracts Tribunal. Sweet and Maxwell.

New Engineering Contract, 3rd edition (NEC3). Thomas Telford Publishing.

Project Partnering Contract 2000 (PPC 2000). Association of Consultant Architects.

Term Partnering Contract 2005 (TPC 2005). Association of Consultant Architects.

Index

adjudication 11
'after the event' (ATE) insurance 7
agreement, formal 22–3, 36, 73–6
alternative dispute resolution (ADR) 9–12
arbitration 11, 57–8
Arb-Med/Adj-Med 12
assistant mediators 26
'authority to settle' 25–6

'bottom lines' 34
briefing 21–2

case law 67–72
case summary preparation 21–2
collaborative working 53–4
co-mediation 21
conciliation 9–10
conditional agreement 37
conditional fee agreements (CFA) 6–7
consultants 25
contract risks 50–1
contractors 25
contracts
    collaborative working 53–4
    dispute boards 58–60
    dispute resolution clauses 54–6
    partnering 53–4
    risk management 50–1
costs
    of conflict 49–50
    litigation 5
    mediation 23–4

deadlock prevention 34–5
dispute boards 58–60, 62

dispute prevention 12, 50–4
dispute resolution clauses 54–6
dispute resolution methods 9–12
documentation
    agreement, formal 22–3, 36, 73–6
    briefing 21–2
    contract 54–6

early neutral evaluation 10
expert determination 11
expert opinions 24

failure to settle 37, 57–8
fees 23–4
first offers 33
formal agreement 22–3, 36, 73–6

indemnity costs 6
independent experts 11, 24
interim agreement 37

legal representation 25
litigation
    versus arbitration 57–8
    costs 4–6
litigation risk 30–2, 50–1

Med-Arb/Med-Ad 11–12
mediation
    defined 9, 12
    key features 12–13
    preparing for 17–28
    process 29–36
    timing 18–19
mediators 19–21

meetings 29–36
model settlement agreement 73–6
multiparty cases 21, 27, 60

negotiation 13–15, 32–6
neutral fact finding 10
'no win, no fee' 6–7

ombudsman 11
out of court settlements 3–5

Part 36 offers 3–5
partnering 52–3
PFI contracts 56–7
pre-mediation contact 26–7
private meetings 13, 30

project mediation 60–2 (*see also* contracts)

refusals to mediate 67–72
'relevant period' 3–4
representatives 24
risk management 50–1

settlement offers 3–5
site visits 23
standard basis costs 6

tiered dispute resolution 54–6
Tomlin order 36, 74

'without prejudice' 13, 22
working groups 35–6